Chains and Rings

Brian Ratcliff

Series editor
Fred Webber

PUBLISHED BY THE PRESS SYNDICATE OF THE UNIVERSITY OF CAMBRIDGE
The Pitt Building, Trumpington Street, Cambridge CB2 1RP, United Kingdom

CAMBRIDGE UNIVERSITY PRESS
The Edinburgh Building, Cambridge CB2 2RU, United Kingdom
40 West 20th Street, New York, NY 10011-4211, USA
10 Stamford Road, Oakleigh, Melbourne 3166, Australia

First published 1996
Reprinted 1996

Printed in the United Kingdom at the University Press, Cambridge

A catalogue record for this book is available from the British Library

ISBN 0 521 42205 1 paperback

Designed and produced by Gecko Ltd, Bicester, Oxon

This book is one of a series produced to support
individual modules within the Cambridge Modular
Sciences scheme. Teachers should note that written
examinations will be set on the content of each module as
defined in the syllabus. This book is the author's
interpretation of the module.

Front cover photograph: View of the reactor towers of a
chemical production facility after sunset. Photographed at
Runcorn, Cheshire. Martin Bond/Science Photo Library

Contents

Acknowledgements

1, Ann Ronan at Image Select; 4, Barry Mayes/Life File; 5, 6, *9t*, 14, courtesy of AgrEvo UK Ltd; *9b*, courtesy of Chiroscience; 11, 12, 13, 24, *26c*, *tr*, *28t*, 29, *31t*, 33, 35, 41, 47, 48, 49, 51, 53, *54tl*, 60, 61, 67, 69, 70, 78, 79, 80, *85l*, Andrew Lambert; *20t*, courtesy of Chemical Industries Association; *20c*, courtesy of BP; *20b*, *87tl*, Robert Hartness; 21, Shell Photo Service; 22, Budd Titlow/f/Stop Pictures Inc.; *23t*, Louise Oldroyd/ Life File; *23b*, Johnson Matthey; *26l*, Images; *26br*, *31cb*, *b*, 42, *54b*, *58t*, *br*, *62r*, 64, 65, *76b*, 92, 95, Michael Brooke; *28bl*, 30, *54tr*, *62l*, 68, courtesy of Chemical Industry Education Centre; *31ct*, Dan Sams/A–Z Botanical Collection Ltd; 38, NASA/Science Photo Library; 43, courtesy of Civil Aviation Authority, International Fire Training Centre, UK and Robert Hartness; 45, H. Schmidbauer/Britstock-IFA; *58c*, Alan Gould/ A–Z Botanical Collection Ltd; *58bl*, *72r*, Wildlife Matters/Garden Matters; *72l*, courtesy of Lever Brothers Ltd; 75, Rafi Ben-Shahar/Oxford Scientific Films; *76t*, A. Barrington Brown/Science Photo Library; *85tr*, Vandystadt/Yann Guichaoua/ Allsport; *85br*, Collections/Shout; *87tl*, courtesy of ICI; *87tr*, James Holmes/Zedcor/Science Photo Library; *87b*, Britstock-IFA/Amadeus; 88, courtesy of ICI; 89, courtesy of James Evans

Chapter one

Basic concepts

By the end of this chapter you should be able to:

1 interpret and use the nomenclature, general formulae and displayed formulae of the following classes of compound: **a** alkanes (including cycloalkanes), alkenes and arenes, **b** halogenoalkanes and halogenoarenes, **c** alcohols (including primary, secondary and tertiary alcohols) and phenols, **d** aldehydes and ketones, **e** carboxylic acids, acyl chlorides and esters, **f** amines (primary only), amides and nitriles;

2 interpret and use the following terminology associated with organic compounds and reactions: **a** *homologous series*, **b** *functional group*, **c** *homolytic* and *heterolytic fission*, **d** *free radical, initiation, propagation* and *termination*, **e** *nucleophile, electrophile* and *inductive effect*, **f** *addition, substitution, elimination* and *hydrolysis*, **g** *oxidation* and *reduction*, **h** *isomerism* (*structural, stereochemical* (*cis–trans* and *optical*)) and *chirality*;

3 describe structural isomerism and the factors which give rise to this phenomenon;

4 describe *cis–trans* isomerism in alkenes;

5 explain what is meant by a *chiral centre* and how such a centre gives rise to optical isomerism;

6 determine the possible isomers for an organic molecule of known molecular formula;

7 identify chiral centres and/or *cis–trans* isomerism in a molecule of given structural formula.

● *Figure 1.1* Friedrich Wöhler made the organic compound urea from an inorganic source. This dispelled the theory that all organic compounds originated from living organisms.

Chains and Rings seeks to provide you with a framework for the study of *organic* chemistry. Organic chemistry includes the study of compounds containing carbon and hydrogen only (that is, hydrocarbons) and of compounds containing other elements in addition to carbon and hydrogen. Such compounds were originally described as organic as they were all believed to be derived from living organisms. Although this idea was dispelled by the synthesis of urea from an inorganic compound, ammonium cyanate, (by the German chemist Friedrich Wöhler in 1828, *figure 1.1*) we still use the term 'organic'.

Organic chemistry is a large subject, mainly because one of its 'essential ingredients', carbon, forms a much greater number and variety of compounds than any other element. Over 90% of known compounds contain carbon, despite the existence of several elements with much greater natural abundance.

Organic chemistry can be studied in a particularly structured and systematic manner because each different group of atoms that becomes attached to carbon has its own characteristic set of reactions. Chemists refer to these different groups of atoms as **functional groups**. In *Foundation Chemistry*, you studied the reactions of the alkene functional group (>C=C<). The functional groups that you will study in *Chains and Rings* are shown in *table 1.1*.

Table 1.1 provides you with the classes and structures of these functional groups. An example is also provided of a simple molecule containing each functional group. Each functional group gives rise to a **homologous series**. For example, the alcohol functional group gives rise to the homologous series of alcohols. The first four of these are

Class of functional group	Structure of functional group	Names of example(s)	Structural formula(e) of example(s)
alkenes	$\diagdown_{/}C=C_{\diagdown}^{/}$	ethene	$CH_2=CH_2$
arenes	(benzene ring)	benzene	(benzene ring)
halogenoalkanes and halogenoarenes	–X, where X = F, Cl, Br, I	chloromethane, chlorobenzene	CH_3Cl, C_6H_5Cl
alcohols and phenols	–OH	methanol, phenol	CH_3OH, C_6H_5OH
ethers	C–O–C	methoxymethane	CH_3OCH_3
aldehydes	$-C\overset{O}{\underset{H}{\big\|}}$	ethanal	CH_3CHO
ketones	$-C-C\overset{O}{\big\|}$	propanone	CH_3COCH_3
carboxylic acids	$-C\overset{O}{\underset{OH}{\big\|}}$	ethanoic acid	CH_3COOH
acyl chlorides	$-C\overset{O}{\underset{Cl}{\big\|}}$	ethanoyl chloride	CH_3COCl
esters	$-C\overset{O}{\underset{O-C}{\big\|}}$	ethyl ethanoate	$CH_3COOC_2H_5$
amines	$-NH_2$	methylamine	CH_3NH_2
amides	$-C\overset{O}{\underset{NH_2}{\big\|}}$	ethanamide	CH_3CONH_2
nitriles	$-C\equiv N$	ethanenitrile	CH_3CN

● **Table 1.1** Functional groups

methanol (CH_3OH), ethanol (CH_3CH_2OH), propan-1-ol ($CH_3CH_2CH_2OH$) and butan-1-ol ($CH_3CH_2CH_2CH_2OH$). The members of a homologous series all have similar chemical properties.

Organic compounds are also classified as either aliphatic or aromatic. **Aromatic** compounds contain one or more arene rings; all other organic compounds are **aliphatic.**

Chemists use different types of formulae to represent organic molecules. **A general formula** may be written for each homologous series. For example, the general formula of the aliphatic alcohols is $C_nH_{2n+1}OH$ (where n is the number of carbon atoms present). **Empirical formulae** are determined by experiments, but they give no indication of structure. The **molecular formula** of a compound is useful when, for example, you need to calculate its molecular mass. **Structural formulae** are particularly useful when writing equations involving aliphatic compounds. **Skeletal formulae** are the clearest and easiest way to represent cyclic compounds in equations. **Displayed formulae** (sometimes called full structural formulae) are useful in checking that you have included the correct number of atoms and bonds. You will often be called upon to provide displayed formulae in your examination answers. However, remember that they do give a completely false impression of the shapes of the molecules concerned. Shapes are best represented using **three-dimensional formulae.** Examples of these types of formulae for the amino acid phenylalanine are shown in *figure 1.2*. Phenylalanine is a common, naturally occurring amino acid.

SAQ 1.1

Represent the compound 2-chloro-2-methylbutane by means of the following types of formulae: **a** displayed, **b** structural, **c** skeletal, **d** molecular, **e** three-dimensional.

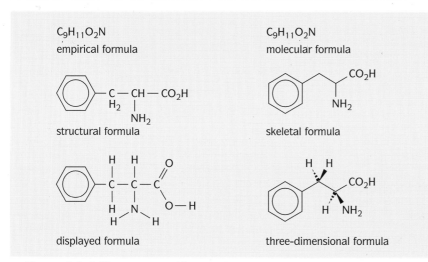

$C_9H_{11}O_2N$
empirical formula

structural formula

displayed formula

$C_9H_{11}O_2N$
molecular formula

skeletal formula

three-dimensional formula

● **Figure 1.2** Different types of formula for phenylalanine. Note that the skeletal form of the phenyl ring ($-C_6H_5$) is acceptable in all of these formulae.

Figure 1.3 shows a range of naturally occurring molecules. They are computer-produced images of ball-and-stick molecular models. In such models, atoms are shown as spheres with radii proportional to the atomic radii of the elements involved. A single bond is represented by a rod and a double bond by two rods. Different elements are distinguished by colour. The colours used are shown in *table 1.2*.

SAQ 1.2

Draw the structural formulae for the molecules shown in *figure 1.3*. Identify and label the functional groups present.

Colour	Element
white	hydrogen
dark grey	carbon
red	oxygen
blue	nitrogen
yellow-green	fluorine
green	chlorine
orange-brown	bromine
brown	iodine
violet	phosphorus
pale yellow	sulphur

● **Table 1.2** The colours used for elements in molecular models

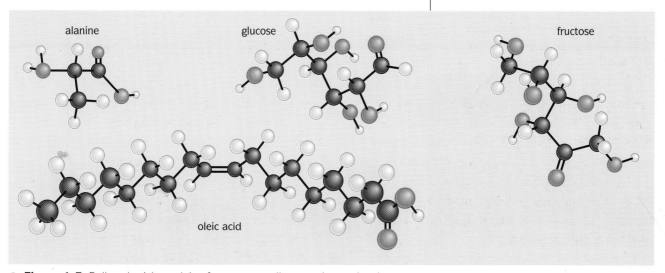

alanine

glucose

fructose

oleic acid

● **Figure 1.3** Ball-and-stick models of some naturally occurring molecules.

Various computer-produced images of molecular models will be used where appropriate throughout this book. Another type that will be used is a space-filling model. In space-filling models, atoms are shown including the space occupied by their electron orbitals. As their orbitals overlap significantly, a

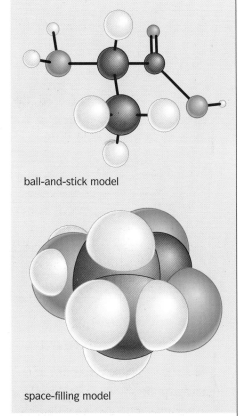

ball-and-stick model

space-filling model

● **Figure 1.4** Different model types for alanine.

● **Figure 1.5** Fermentation vessels in the Carlsberg brewery.

very different image to the ball-and-stick image results. *Figure 1.4* shows these two types of model for alanine.

We shall now discuss three types of formulae in more detail.

Empirical formulae

The determination of the empirical formula of an organic compound involves **combustion analysis**. A known mass of the compound is burned completely in an excess of oxygen. The carbon dioxide and water produced are collected by absorption onto suitable solids, and the masses of these products are measured. From these results we can determine the masses of carbon and of hydrogen in the weighed sample. If oxygen is present this is found by subtracting the masses of the other elements present.

If the compound contains nitrogen, a second sample of known mass is reduced using a mixture of reducing agents. Subsequent treatments drive the nitrogen off as ammonia, the quantity of which is determined by titration with acid. This method was named after Kjeldahl (pronounced Keldale) who used it in 1883 for the analysis of the grain for Carlsberg lager *(figure 1.5)*.

Let us now look at how the empirical formula of an amino acid is determined. We shall assume, for example, that 0.10000 g of an amino acid produced 0.11710 g of carbon dioxide and 0.05992 g of water, and that in a Kjeldahl determination of nitrogen, a second 0.10000 g of the amino acid produced 0.02264 g of ammonia. Determine the empirical formula of the amino acid.

We first calculate the masses of carbon, hydrogen and nitrogen in 0.10000 g of the amino acid:

As 12 g of carbon are present in 1 mol (= 44 g) CO_2,

$$\text{mass of carbon in } 0.11710\,\text{g of } CO_2 = \frac{12}{44} \times 0.11710\,\text{g}$$
$$= 0.03194\,\text{g}$$
$$= \text{mass of carbon in the amino acid}$$

As 2 g of hydrogen are present in 1 mol (= 18 g) H_2O,

$$\text{mass of hydrogen in } 0.05992\,\text{g of } H_2O = \frac{2}{18} \times 0.05992\,\text{g}$$
$$= 0.00666\,\text{g}$$
$$= \text{mass of hydrogen in the amino acid}$$

As 14 g of nitrogen are present in 1 mol (= 17 g) NH_3,

$$\text{mass of nitrogen in } 0.02264\,\text{g of } NH_3 = \frac{14}{17} \times 0.02264\,\text{g}$$
$$= 0.01864\,\text{g}$$

Hence

$$\text{mass of oxygen in the amino acid} = (0.10000 - 0.03194 - 0.00666 - 0.01864)\,g$$

$$= 0.04276\,g$$

	C	H	O	N
Mass/g	0.03194	0.00666	0.04276	0.01864
Amount/ mol	0.03194/12 $= 2.66 \times 10^{-3}$	0.00666/1 $= 6.66 \times 10^{-3}$	0.04276/16 $= 2.67 \times 10^{-3}$	0.01864/14 $= 1.33 \times 10^{-3}$

Divide by the smallest amount to give whole numbers:

Atoms/ mol	2	5	2	1

Hence the empirical formula is $C_2H_5O_2N$.

SAQ 1.3

A 0.2000 g sample of an organic compound, **W**, was analysed by combustion analysis. 0.4800 g of carbon dioxide and 0.1636 g of water were obtained. A second 0.2000 g sample of **W** produced 0.0618 g of ammonia in a Kjeldahl analysis. Use this data to show that **W** contains only carbon, hydrogen and nitrogen and calculate the empirical formula of **W**.

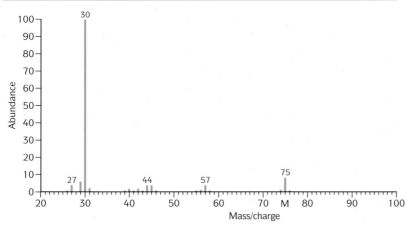

● **Figure 1.6** The mass spectrum of glycine.

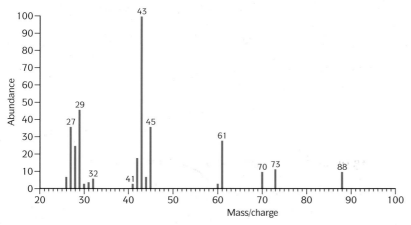

● **Figure 1.7** The mass spectrum of ester **Y**.

Molecular formulae

Molecular masses are found using a mass spectrometer. The mass spectrum of the amino acid in the example of an empirical formula calculation is shown in *figure 1.6*. This spectrum shows a molecular ion peak, labelled **M**, at a mass/charge ratio of 75. Hence the M_r of the amino acid is 75.

We can now find the molecular formula for this amino acid:

$C_2H_5O_2N$ has M_r
$= 24 + 5 + 32 + 14 = 75.$

As M_r of the amino acid is 75, the molecular formula of the compound is also $C_2H_5O_2N$.

SAQ 1.4

An ester **Y** has the empirical formula C_2H_4O. The mass spectrum of the ester is shown in *figure 1.7*. Use the mass spectrum to obtain the molecular mass of the ester **Y**. What is the molecular formula of the ester?

Structural formulae

The mass spectrum of our amino acid sample shows several peaks at lower mass/charge ratios than the molecular ion. These peaks constitute the **fragmentation pattern** for the molecule. **Fragment ions** in this example occur at the following mass/charge ratios and correspond to the fragment ions shown:

Mass/charge ratio	Fragment ion
30	$H_2N-CH_2^+$
28	CO^+
17	OH^+

These fragment ions may be pieced together, like a jigsaw puzzle, to give the structural formula of the amino acid:

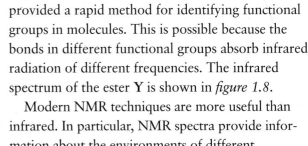

SAQ 1.5

Suggest structures for the fragment ions **A**, **B** and **C**, which occur in the mass spectrum of the ester **Y** *(figure 1.7)* at mass/charge ratios 29, 43 and 45 respectively.

There are other spectroscopic methods for finding the structure of a compound. These include infrared spectroscopy and nuclear magnetic resonance spectroscopy (NMR). Although these are beyond the scope of this book (they are studied in *Methods of Analysis and Detection*), they are worth discussing briefly as they are widely used in industrial and university laboratories.

For many years infrared spectroscopy has provided a rapid method for identifying functional groups in molecules. This is possible because the bonds in different functional groups absorb infrared radiation of different frequencies. The infrared spectrum of the ester **Y** is shown in *figure 1.8*.

Modern NMR techniques are more useful than infrared. In particular, NMR spectra provide information about the environments of different hydrogen atoms in a molecule. This information is not easily available from infrared spectra. In recent years the introduction of more powerful superconducting magnets has enabled NMR to provide much more detail concerning the structure of a compound. As NMR spectra are also produced quickly, this has led to a decline in the use of infrared spectroscopy for finding structural formulae.

The NMR spectrum of the ester **Y** is shown in *figure 1.9*.

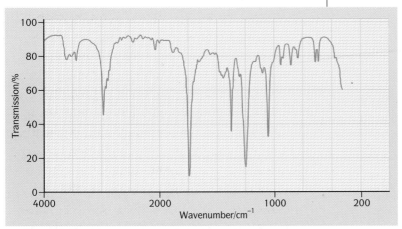

● *Figure 1.8* The infrared spectrum of ester **Y**. The strong absorption at $1720 \, cm^{-1}$ is characteristic of an ester carbonyl group.

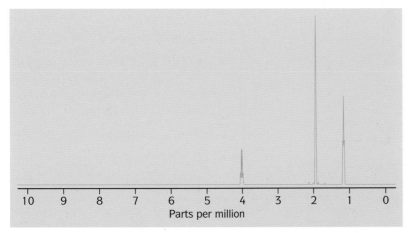

● *Figure 1.9* The nuclear magnetic resonance spectrum of ester **Y**.

Isomerism

Most organic compounds have a molecular formula that is the same as one or more other compounds. This property is called isomerism. **Isomers have the same molecular formula but the atoms are arranged in different ways.** Isomerism arises for a number of reasons, including the ability of carbon to bond to itself and to most other elements in the Periodic Table. The atoms present in a given molecular formula may be treated rather like Lego®, in that a given number of different pieces may be put together in a variety of ways.

Structural isomerism

Structural isomerism describes the situation where chemicals of the same formula behave differently because the structures are different.

For example, the atoms of butane, C_4H_{10}, can be put together in two different ways. Try building models of these two isomers (or use a molecular modelling program on a computer). The two isomers behave in a very similar way chemically. The most noticeable difference in their properties is in their boiling points. One isomer is more compact. This reduces the intermolecular forces as the molecules cannot approach each other so closely. This isomer has a boiling point of $-11.6°C$. The isomer which is less compact has a boiling point of $-0.4°C$. The displayed formulae and the names of these two structural isomers are:

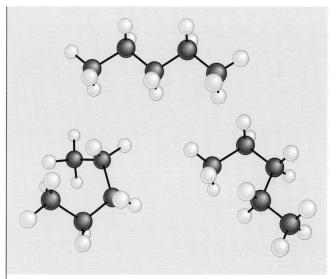
● **Figure 1.11** Models showing the flexibility of pentane. These forms are the same molecule, they are not isomers. The flexibility is due to the free rotation about the C–C single bond.

butane

methylpropane

SAQ 1.6

Copy the displayed formulae of the structural isomers of butane. Label each isomer with its appropriate boiling point.

The molecular formula C_2H_6O provides a very different example of structural isomerism. It has two isomers: ethanol, C_2H_5OH, and methoxymethane, CH_3OCH_3. Molecular models of these two isomers are shown in *figure 1.10*. Ethanol is an alcohol whilst methoxymethane is the simplest member of the homologous series of ethers. As they contain different functional groups, they have very different chemical and physical properties. Ethanol is able to form intermolecular hydrogen bonds; methoxymethane has weaker dipole–dipole

intermolecular forces. Consequently the boiling point of ethanol ($78.5°C$) is considerably higher than that of methoxymethane ($-25°C$). Alcohols have a variety of different reactions. Ethers, apart from being highly flammable, are relatively inert.

It is quite easy to mistake the flexibility of molecular structures for isomerism. For example, if you build a model of pentane, C_5H_{10}, you will find it is very flexible (*figure 1.11* shows three of the possibilities). The flexibility of a carbon chain arises because atoms can rotate freely about a carbon–carbon single bond. You should be careful when drawing displayed formulae of isomers not to include structures such as:

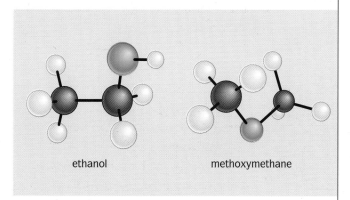
ethanol   methoxymethane

● **Figure 1.10** Structural isomers of C_2H_6O.

These are all the same molecule; compare the displayed formula with the models in *figure 1.11*. Displayed formulae give a false impression of these structures. Remember that there is a tetrahedral arrangement of atoms round each carbon atom (with bond angles of 109.5°, not 90° as in displayed formulae).

SAQ 1.7

Draw the displayed formulae for all the structural isomers of hexane.

Stereoisomerism

In stereoisomerism, the same atoms are joined to each other in different spatial arrangements. Geometric and optical isomerism are two types of this stereoisomerism.

Geometric (or *cis–trans*) isomerism

Whilst atoms on either side of a carbon–carbon single bond can rotate freely, those either side of a carbon–carbon double bond cannot. Try making models of but-2-ene, $CH_3CH=CHCH_3$. Two geometric (or *cis–trans*) isomers are possible. You should obtain models similar to those shown in *figure 1.12*. (In *cis*-but-2-ene, the methyl groups are on the same side of the double bond. In *trans*-but-2-ene, they lie across the double bond.)

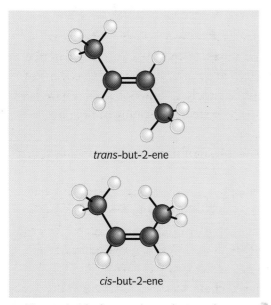

trans-but-2-ene

cis-but-2-ene

● **Figure 1.12** Geometric or *cis–trans* isomers of but-2-ene.

SAQ 1.8

a Draw the geometric isomers of 1,2-dichloroethene, CHCl=CHCl and label them as *cis* or *trans*.

b Copy the following structures and indicate which can exhibit geometric isomerism by drawing the second isomer and labelling the two isomers as *cis* or *trans*.

$$
\begin{array}{cccc}
\underset{H}{\overset{Br}{>}}C=C\underset{H}{\overset{Br}{<}} &
\underset{H}{\overset{Br}{>}}C=C\underset{H}{\overset{H}{<}} &
\underset{H}{\overset{Br}{>}}C=C\underset{H}{\overset{CH_3}{<}} &
\underset{H}{\overset{Br}{>}}C=C\underset{CH_3}{\overset{CH_3}{<}}
\end{array}
$$

Optical isomerism

The simplest form of optical isomerism occurs when a carbon atom is joined to four different groups. The groups may be arranged in two different ways and the two isomers so formed are mirror images of each other, which cannot be superimposed. Try making models of the amino acid alanine.

$$
H-\underset{\underset{NH_2}{|}}{\overset{\overset{CH_3}{|}}{C}}-CO_2H
$$

If you have made two models that are mirror images of each other, you will find that you are unable to superimpose them so that they match. Molecular models of the two optical isomers of alanine are shown in *figure 1.13*.

Molecules that are mirror images, which cannot be superimposed, are known as **chiral** molecules. The name comes from the Greek for hand. Place your hands together with the palms in contact.

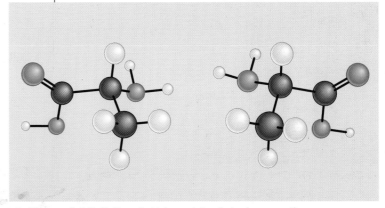

● **Figure 1.13** Ball-and-stick models of alanine enantiomers.

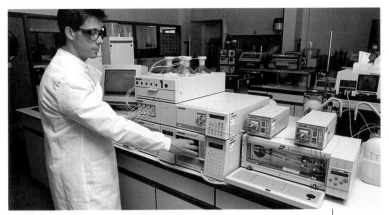

● *Figure 1.14* High-performance liquid chromatography equipment.

Hands are mirror images of each other. Place one hand on top of the other with both palms uppermost. Your thumbs are now on opposite sides. Like chiral molecules, hands cannot be superimposed. Optical isomerism is often referred to as **chirality**. The carbon atom which carries four different groups is a **chiral centre.**

Optical isomers are also called **enantiomers**. Many of the molecules found in living organisms exist as enantiomers. Usually only one of the enantiomers is biochemically active. This is not surprising when you consider the shape selectivity of, for example, enzymes. Medicines that have chiral molecules may need to be administered as a pure enantiomer. Synthetic organic reactions usually result in a mixture containing equal

● *Figure 1.15* Ellen on work experience at Chiroscience, a company that specialises in making pure enantiomers of medicines.

amounts of both isomers (a **racemic mixture**). Purification of such mixtures can be done by crystallisation with a chiral acid or base. However, new separation techniques such as chiral high-performance liquid chromatography are enabling much better separations (*figure 1.14*). To avoid expensive separation techniques, a few 'leading technology' companies are now making pure enantiomers using synthetic routes which produce only the required enantiomer (*figure 1.15*).

SAQ 1.9

a Draw the enantiomers of bromochlorofluoromethane.

b Copy the following formulae and mark the chiral centres with an asterisk:

$$CH_3CH_2CHBrCH_3$$

Naming organic compounds

The names used in this section are known as **systematic** names. Such names precisely describe the structure of a molecule and enable chemists to communicate clearly. International rules have been agreed for the systematic naming of organic compounds.

The basic rules for naming hydrocarbons are as follows.

1 The number of carbon atoms in the longest chain provides the stem of the name. Simple alkanes consist entirely of unbranched chains of carbon atoms. They are named by adding -ane to this stem, as shown in *table 1.3*.

2 Branched-chain alkanes are named in the same way. The name given to the longest continuous carbon chain is then prefixed by the names of

Structural formula	Number of carbon atoms in longest chain	Stem	Name
CH_4	1	meth-	methane
C_2H_6	2	eth-	ethane
C_3H_8	3	prop-	propane
C_4H_{10}	4	but-	butane
C_5H_{12}	5	pent-	pentane
C_6H_{14}	6	hex-	hexane
C_7H_{16}	7	hept-	heptane
C_8H_{18}	8	oct-	octane
C_9H_{20}	9	non-	nonane
$C_{10}H_{22}$	10	dec-	decane
$C_{20}H_{42}$	20	eicos-	eicosane

● **Table 1.3** Naming simple alkanes

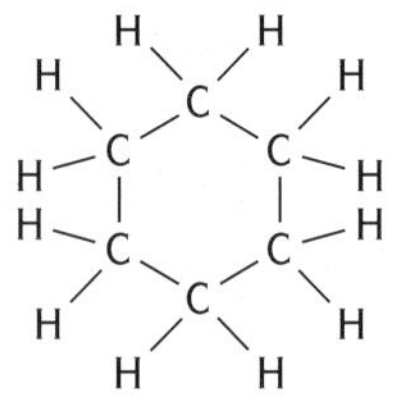

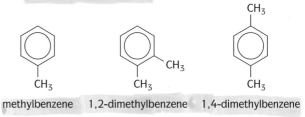

displayed formula   skeletal formula

the shorter side-chains. The same stems are used with the suffix -yl. Hence CH_3- is methyl (often called a methyl group). In general, such groups are called alkyl groups. The position of an alkyl group is indicated by a number. The carbon atoms in the longest carbon chain are numbered from one end of the chain. Numbering starts from the end which produces the lowest possible numbers for the side chains. For example, this molecule

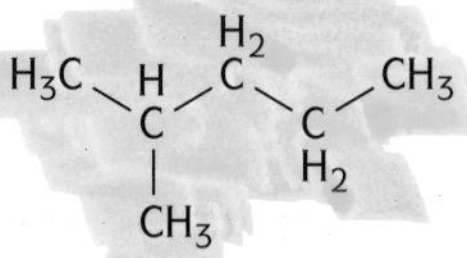

is 2-methylpentane, not 4-methylpentane.

3 Each side-chain must be included in the name. If there are several identical side-chains, the name is prefixed by di-, tri- etc. For example, 2,2,3-trimethyl- indicates that there are three methyl groups, two on the second and one on the third carbon atom of the longest chain. Note that numbers are separated by commas whilst a number and a letter are separated by a hyphen.

4 Where different alkyl groups are present, they are placed in alphabetical order, as in 3-ethyl-2-methylpentane.

5 Compounds containing a ring of carbon atoms are prefixed by cyclo-. Cyclohexane is represented by:

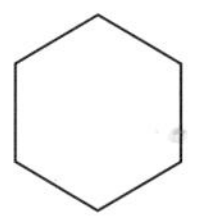

6 Hydrocarbons containing one double bond are called **alkenes**. The same stems are used, but they are followed by -ene. The position of an alkene double bond is indicated by the lower number of the two carbon atoms involved. This number is placed between the stem and -ene. Hence $CH_3CH=CHCH_3$ is but-2-ene.

7 The simplest arene is benzene. When one alkyl group is attached to a benzene ring, a number is not needed because all the carbon atoms are equivalent. Two or more groups will require a number. For example:

methylbenzene   1,2-dimethylbenzene   1,4-dimethylbenzene

8 Halogeno or nitro compounds are named in the same way as alkyl-substituted alkanes or arenes:

$CH_3CH_2CHBrCH_3$

2-bromobutane   1,3-dinitrobenzene

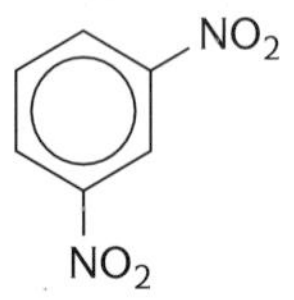

9 Aliphatic alcohols and ketones are named in a similar way to alkenes:

$CH_3CH_2CH_2OH$ $CH_3CH_2COCH_2CH_3$

propan-1-ol   pentan-3-one

10 Aliphatic aldehyde and carboxylic acid groups are at the end of a carbon chain, so they do not need a number. There is only one possible butanoic acid, $CH_3CH_2CH_2COOH$, or butanal, $CH_3CH_2CH_2CHO$. The names of

ketones, aldehydes, carboxylic acids and nitriles include the carbon atom in the functional group in the stem. Hence CH_3COOH is ethanoic acid and CH_3CN is ethanenitrile.

11 Amines are named using the alkyl- or aryl-prefix followed by -amine. Hence $CH_3CH_2NH_2$ is ethylamine.

SAQ 1.10

a   Name the following compounds:

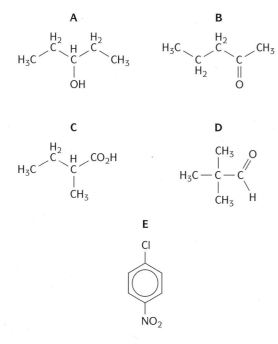

b   Draw structural formulae for the following compounds:
   (i) propanal; (ii) propan-2-ol;
   (iii) 2-methylpentan-3-one; (iv) propylamine;
   (v) propanenitrile; (vi) 2,4,6-trinitromethylbenzene.

Practical techniques

Many organic reactions proceed slowly. They often require heating for a period of time. As the reaction mixtures required often contain volatile reactants or solvent, the heating must be carried out under **reflux**: a condenser is placed in the neck of the reaction flask so that the volatile components are condensed and returned to the flask. *Figure 1.16* illustrates the arrangement together with a cross-section diagram (of the type you might reproduce in an examination answer). Note that the water flows into the condenser at the

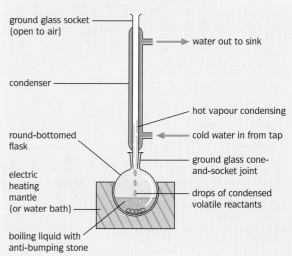

● *Figure 1.16* The apparatus for carrying out a reaction under reflux.

lower (hotter end). This provides the most rapid cooling of the vapour back to liquid. The liquid which is returned to the flask is still close to its boiling point.

The time required for the reflux period will depend on the rate of the reaction. Many reactions require a short period of reflux (perhaps 10 to 30 minutes). Some reactions may require as long as 24 hours. The use of thermostatically controlled heating mantles (*figure 1.16*) allows long refluxes to be carried out safely overnight.

After reflux, the reaction mixture is likely to consist of an equilibrium mixture containing both reactant and product molecules. These may usually be separated by a simple distillation. A photograph

● **Figure 1.17** The apparatus for a distillation.

of distillation apparatus appears in *figure 1.17*. Compare the water flow with the flow for the reflux apparatus. For distillation, although the cold water enters at the lower end of the condenser (as with reflux), this entry point is further from the flask. The water not only condenses the vapour, but also cools the liquid to bring it close to room temperature.

After distillation, further purification may require washing the impure product with water in a separating funnel (*figure 1.18*). This enables the

● **Figure 1.18** Sarah is carrying out an analysis of the concentration of lead in water. Lead forms a coloured complex ion when reacted with dithizone. The intensity of the colour is proportional to the concentration of lead. The separating funnel enables the organic layer to be separated from the aqueous layer.

separation of immiscible liquids. After washing in a separating funnel, the liquid may require drying. It is placed in a stoppered flask together with an anhydrous salt such as calcium chloride. This absorbs excess water. After drying, the liquid will require filtering and redistilling.

Where the product is a solid, distillation is inappropriate. Solid products may crystallise in the reaction flask or may be precipitated on pouring the reaction mixture into water. Rapid separation of the solid is achieved by vacuum filtration (*figure 1.19*).

The solid is purified by recrystallisation from a suitable solvent. The aim of recrystallisation is to use just enough hot solvent to completely dissolve

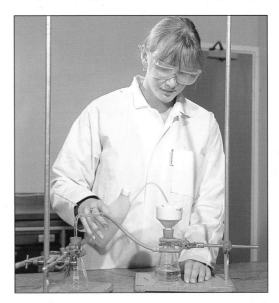

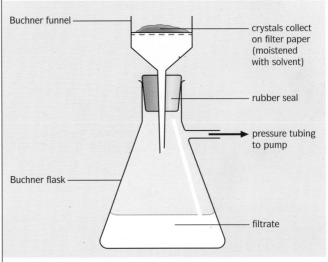

Buchner funnel — crystals collect on filter paper (moistened with solvent)

— rubber seal

— pressure tubing to pump

Buchner flask —

— filtrate

● **Figure 1.19** The apparatus required for a vacuum filtration.

all the solid. On cooling, the product crystallises, leaving impurities in solution. The purity of a compound may be checked by finding its melting point. A pure compound will usually have a sharp melting point (that is, the point from where it begins to soften to where it is completely liquid is a narrow range of temperature (1 or 2 °C)), whereas an impure compound will melt over a larger range of temperature. The melting-point apparatus shown in *figure 1.20* enables the melting of individual crystals to be seen.

Criteria for checking purity

Determination of the melting point of a solid is one method for checking the purity of a product. The boiling point of a liquid may also give some indication of purity. There are many modern techniques for establishing purity. Amongst these methods, the techniques of thin-layer chromatography, gas–liquid chromatography and high-performance liquid chromatography are widely used. Paper chromatography and electrophoresis are also used.

Many of these methods are coupled to spectroscopic techniques. Gas–liquid chromatography is often followed by mass spectroscopy of the separated components. High-performance liquid chromatography and electrophoresis may be followed by ultraviolet or visible spectroscopy of each component. A capillary electrophoresis apparatus is shown in *figure 1.21*, together with a sample print of results showing the spectra of the components using a three-dimensional graph.

Calculation of percentage yields

Organic reactions often give yields much less than 100%. This is hardly surprising when the product is subjected to recrystallisation or distillation. Material is lost each time the product is transferred from one piece of equipment to another. In addition to this problem, many reactions produce equilibrium mixtures.

In order to find the yield of the product, you first calculate the maximum mass of product that you could obtain from the starting material. This may involve a preliminary calculation to decide if one or more of the reagents is in excess. If a reagent is in excess, the other reagent will limit the maximum yield of product. We will use the synthesis of aspirin as an example.

2.0 g of 2-hydroxybenzoic acid is refluxed with 5.5 g of ethanoic anhydride. The products are aspirin and ethanoic acid. The aspirin is easily

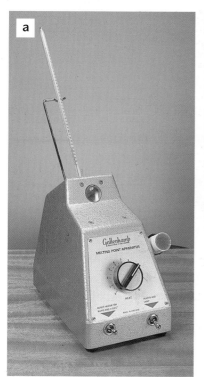

a

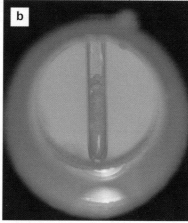

b

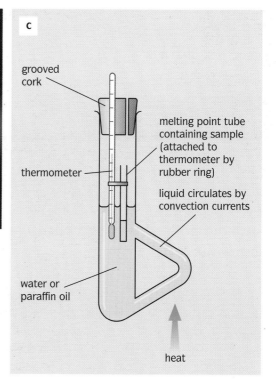

c

● **Figure 1.20**
a A simple apparatus used to determine melting point.
b Close-up of crystals melting in the apparatus.
c Diagram of a Thiele tube apparatus, also used to determine melting point.

grooved cork

melting point tube containing sample (attached to thermometer by rubber ring)

thermometer

liquid circulates by convection currents

water or paraffin oil

heat

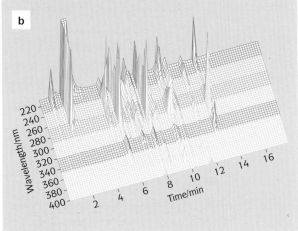

● **Figure 1.21**

a Capillary electrophoresis equipment.

b Capillary electrophoresis enables the separation of organic molecules to take place under the influence of a high voltage. This electrophoretogram shows the retention times for compounds in a mixture; different compounds pass through the capillary tube at different rates. As each compound emerges from the capillary tube, its ultraviolet spectrum is also recorded. The vertical axis shows the absorption of ultraviolet radiation for each compound at certain wavelengths.

separated as a solid. The equation for the reaction, together with the relative molecular masses of the compounds, is:

2-hydroxybenzoic acid
$M_r = 138$
ethanoic anhydride
$M_r = 102$
aspirin
$M_r = 180$

$$\text{Amount of 2-hydroxybenzoic acid used} = \frac{2.0}{138}$$
$$= 0.0145 \, \text{mol}$$

$$\text{Amount of ethanoic anhydride used} = \frac{5.5}{102}$$
$$= 0.54 \, \text{mol}$$

As 0.0145 mol of 2-hydroxybenzoic acid requires only 0.0145 mol of ethanoic anhydride, a large excess of ethanoic anhydride has been used.

The reaction equation shows us that one mole of 2-hydroxybenzoic acid produces one mole of aspirin.

Hence maximum yield of aspirin

$$= \frac{180}{138} \times 2.0 = 2.6 \, \text{g}$$

A student making aspirin whilst studying this module prepared 1.2 g of recrystallised aspirin. His percentage yield was thus

$$\frac{1.2}{2.6} \times 100 = 46\%$$

SAQ 1.11

A student prepared a sample of 1-bromobutane, C_4H_9Br, from 10.0 g of butan-1-ol, C_4H_9OH. After purification she found she had made 12.0 g of 1-bromobutane. What was the percentage yield?

Organising organic reactions

There are several ways of organising the study of organic reactions. You will find each of these helpful in different ways and for various purposes. This book is organised by functional group, so that subsequent chapters of this book provide you with information about the typical reactions of the functional groups. Before you study these reactions, you need to know a little about the general types of reaction that occur.

You should be familiar with **acid–base** and reduction–oxidation (**redox**) reactions. Organic compounds frequently exhibit both these types of reaction. For example, ethanoic acid behaves as a typical acid, forming salts when reacted with alkalis such as aqueous sodium hydroxide:

$$CH_3COOH(aq) + NaOH(aq) \longrightarrow CH_3COONa(aq) + H_2O(l)$$

As with other acid–base reactions, a salt (sodium ethanoate) and water are formed. Ethanol is readily oxidised in air to ethanoic acid (wine or beer soon become oxidised to vinegar if left exposed to the air):

$$CH_3CH_2OH(aq) + O_2(g) \longrightarrow CH_3COOH(aq) + H_2O(l)$$

In this redox reaction, oxygen is reduced to water.

There are several other types of reaction. These are substitution, addition, elimination and hydrolysis.

■ **Substitution** involves replacing an atom (or a group of atoms) by another atom (or group of atoms). For example, the bromine atom in bromoethane is substituted by the –OH group to form ethanol on warming with aqueous sodium hydroxide:

$$CH_3CH_2Br(l) + OH^-(aq) \longrightarrow CH_3CH_2OH(aq) + Br^-(aq)$$

■ **Addition** reactions involve two molecules joining together to form a single new molecule. If ethene and steam are passed over a hot phosphoric acid catalyst, ethanol is produced:

$$CH_2{=}CH_2(g) + H_2O(g) \longrightarrow CH_3CH_2OH(g)$$

■ **Elimination** involves the removal of a molecule from a larger one. The addition of ethene to steam may be reversed by passing ethanol vapour over a hot catalyst such as pumice. A water molecule is eliminated:

$$CH_3CH_2OH(g) \longrightarrow CH_2{=}CH_2(g) + H_2O(g)$$

■ **Hydrolysis** reactions involve breaking covalent bonds by reaction with water. The peptide bonds in proteins are hydrolysed in the presence of acids or enzymes, producing amino acids:

$$protein + water \rightarrow amino\ acids$$

What is a reaction mechanism?

A balanced chemical equation shows the reactants and the products of a chemical change. It provides no information about the reaction pathway. The **reaction pathway** will include details of intermediate chemical species (molecules, radicals or ions), which have a transient existence between reactants and products. The **activation energy** for a reaction is the energy required to form these transient species *(figure 1.22a)*. **Catalysts** are frequently used in reactions to increase the rate of reaction. They do this by providing an alternative reaction pathway with a lower activation energy *(figure 1.22b)*.

If a reaction pathway with a lower activation energy is found, more molecules will have sufficient kinetic energy to react.

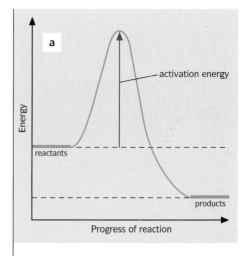

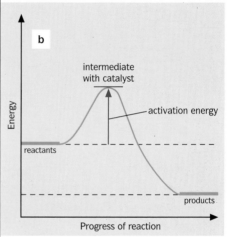

● *Figure 1.22* Activation energy diagrams for a reaction:
a without a catalyst;
b with a catalyst.

Catalysts take part in the reaction mechanism, but they are recovered unchanged at the end of the reaction. Hence the catalyst does not appear in the balanced chemical equation for the reaction.

The mechanism is described using equations for the steps involved. You will meet the following organic mechanisms in this book:

■ free-radical substitution (page 25);

■ electrophilic addition (page 30);

- electrophilic substitution (page 34);
- nucleophilic substitution (page 40);
- nucleophilic addition (page 60).

The terms free-radical, electrophilic and nucleophilic refer to the nature of the attacking species (the reactant that starts a reaction by 'attacking' a bond on another reactant) in the reaction. These terms will be explained in the next section.

Breaking bonds in different ways

A covalent bond consists of a pair of electrons lying between the nuclei of two atoms. The negatively charged electrons attract both nuclei, binding them together. Such a bond may be broken in two different ways. We will consider these possibilities for hydrogen chloride. The dot-and-cross diagram for hydrogen chloride is:

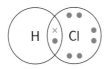

The bond may be broken so that each element takes one of the covalent bond electrons:

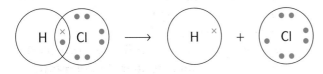

Each element now has a single unpaired electron. (In this example they have also become atoms.) Atoms (or groups of atoms) with unpaired electrons are known as **free radicals**. When a covalent bond is broken to form two free radicals, the process is called **homolytic fission**. If a bonds breaks homolytically, it usually occurs under ultraviolet light or at high temperature.

The movement of *one* electron from a bond is sometimes shown by a *half-headed* curly arrow. Unpaired electrons are represented by a dot. Using half-headed curly arrows and dots for the unpaired electrons, the homolytic fission of bromomethane to form a methyl radical and a bromine radical may be represented as follows:

$$H_3C \overset{\frown\frown}{-} Br \longrightarrow CH_3\bullet + Br\bullet$$

Alternatively, a covalent bond may be broken so that one element takes both covalent bond electrons. Hydrogen chloride would form hydrogen and chloride ions:

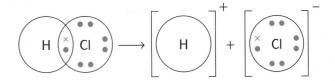

Notice that the more electronegative element takes both electrons. When a covalent bond is broken to form two oppositely charged ions, the process is called **heterolytic fission**. The bond in hydrogen chloride breaks heterolytically when the gas dissolves in water to form hydrochloric acid.

The movement of *two* electrons from the bond to the same atom is sometimes shown by a *full-headed* curly arrow. Using full-headed curly arrows, the heterolytic fission of bromomethane to form a positive methyl ion and a bromide ion may be represented as follows:

$$H_3C \overset{\frown}{-} Br \longrightarrow CH_3^+ + Br^-$$

Positively charged ions like CH_3^+ are known as **carbocations**. (An ion such as CH_3^- is known as a **carbanion**.)

Free radicals, carbocations and carbanions are all highly reactive species. They react with molecules, causing covalent bonds to break and new covalent bonds to form.

Carbocations and carbanions are examples of reagents known as electrophiles and nucleophiles respectively. An **electrophile** (electron-lover) is a reagent which is attracted to an electron-rich centre, leading to the formation of a new covalent bond between the electrophile and the molecule under attack. Electrophiles must be capable of accepting a pair of electrons. A **nucleophile** (nucleus-lover) is a reagent attracted to a centre with a partial positive charge, leading to the formation of a new covalent bond between the nucleophile and the molecule under attack. Nucleophiles must possess a lone-pair of electrons for this new bond.

SAQ 1.12

Draw dot-and-cross diagrams for the following species: $Br•$, Cl^-, CH_3^+, CH_3^-, $CH_3•$, NH_3, BF_3. Classify them as free radicals, electrophiles or nucleophiles. What do you notice about the outer electron shells of free radicals, electrophiles and nucleophiles?

Both electrophilic and nucleophilic reactions are influenced by the electron charge on the atom under attack. This charge is dependent on the relative electronegativities of the atom under attack and its neighbours. It may also be influenced by effects which are transmitted through the bonding molecular orbitals. These effects may involve electrons in delocalised π orbitals or in σ orbitals. For example, the **inductive effect** is a movement of electron charge from one atom towards another in a σ bond. Hence the attraction of an electronegative atom, such as chlorine, for the electrons in a σ bond to carbon will reduce the electron charge in the bond. The halogen atom exerts a *negative* inductive effect. Electron charge is transmitted *away* from alkyl groups towards the halogen. Alkyl groups thus have a *positive* inductive effect.

Questions

1 A compound **A** has the following percentage composition, by mass: C, 51.9; Cl, 38.4; H, 9.7. The molecular formula of **A** is the same as its empirical formula.
Calculate the empirical formula of **A**.
What additional information is needed to show that the molecular formula and empirical formula are identical?

2 The equation for the reaction between salicylic acid and ethanoyl chloride to produce aspirin is as follows:

2-hydroxybenzoic acid   aspirin

In an experiment to prepare aspirin, 100 g of salicylic acid were used and yielded 117 g of pure aspirin. Calculate:
a the M_r of salicylic acid;
b the M_r of aspirin;
c how many moles of salicylic acid were used;
d the maximum amount, in moles, of aspirin that could be produced;
e the maximum mass of aspirin that could be produced;
f the percentage yield of the reaction.

3 Give an account of the various types of isomerism. In your answer, explain how the various types of isomerism arise, and give a named example of each type.

SUMMARY

- All organic compounds contain carbon and hydrogen. Most organic compounds also contain other elements, such as oxygen, nitrogen and chlorine.

- Functional groups, which have their own characteristic reactions, are attached to the hydrocarbon framework of an organic molecule. Alkenes, arenes, halogen atoms, alcohols, aldehydes and ketones, carboxylic acids, esters, acyl chlorides, amines, amides and nitriles are examples of functional groups.

- Chemists use a wide variety of formulae to represent organic molecules. These include general, empirical, molecular, structural, skeletal, displayed and three-dimensional formulae.

- Various types of molecular models (ball-and-stick, space-filling) are used to visualise organic molecules.

- The empirical formula of an organic compound is found by combustion analysis. The molecular mass is found from the molecular ion in the mass spectrum. The molecular mass and empirical formula enable the molecular formula to be established. Use of the fragmentation pattern from the mass spectrum enables a structural formula to be found. Nuclear magnetic resonance and infrared spectroscopy also provide structural information.

- Organic molecules with the same molecular formula but with different structures are called isomers. Three common types of isomerism are structural, *cis–trans* (or geometrical) and optical. Structural isomers have different structural formulae, *cis–trans* isomers have different displayed formulae and optical isomers have different three-dimensional formulae. Optical isomers (or enantiomers) are molecules that are mirror images of each other. They contain one or more chiral carbon atoms.

- Organic molecules are named in a systematic way, related to their structures.

- Practical techniques used in the preparation of organic compounds include reflux, distillation, vacuum filtration, separation of immiscible liquids in a separating funnel and recrystallisation.

- Most organic preparations involve equilibrium reactions and/or lead to losses of product during separation and purification. The percentage yield indicates the proportion of the maximum yield that has been obtained.

- The study of organic reactions is traditionally organised by functional group. Each functional group has its own characteristic reactions.

- Reactions may also be studied by type or by mechanism. Organic compounds may show the following types of reaction: acid–base, redox, substitution, addition, elimination or hydrolysis.

- Reaction mechanisms may involve electrophiles, nucleophiles or free radicals. Each of these reagents is capable of forming a new covalent bond to the atom attacked. Electrophiles attack atoms with a high electron density, nucleophiles attack atoms with a low electron density. Free radicals are highly reactive, attacking any atom with which they are capable of forming a bond.

- Covalent bonds may be broken homolytically to form two free radicals, each with an unpaired electron. Polar bonds will frequently break heterolytically to form one cation and one anion.

- Curly arrows show the movement of electrons in a reaction mechanism. A half-headed curly arrow is used for one electron, a full-headed curly arrow is used for two electrons.

- Electrophiles must be capable of accepting a pair of electrons; nucleophiles must have a lone-pair of electrons available for bond formation.

- The inductive effect describes the transmission of electron density by an atom or group towards (positive inductive effect) or away from (negative inductive effect) another atom.

Chapter two

Hydrocarbons

By the end of this chapter you should be able to:

1 explain the use of crude oil as a source of both aliphatic and aromatic hydrocarbons;

2 describe how 'cracking', re-forming or isomerisation can be used to obtain more useful alkanes and alkenes of lower M_r from larger hydrocarbon molecules;

3 describe the pollutant gases emitted by motor vehicles and their effects on the environment;

4 describe the shapes of the ethane, ethene and benzene molecules;

5 explain the shapes of the ethane, ethene and benzene molecules in terms of σ and π carbon–carbon bonds;

6 predict the shapes of other related molecules;

7 explain the origin of *cis–trans* isomerism in terms of restricted rotation due to the presence of π bonds in alkenes;

8 show awareness of the general unreactivity of alkanes, including towards polar reagents;

9 describe and explain the chemistry of alkanes, as exemplified by reactions of ethane including combustion and substitution, both by chlorine and by bromine;

10 describe and explain the mechanism of free-radical substitution at methyl groups with particular reference to the initiation, propagation and termination reactions;

11 describe and explain the chemistry of alkenes as exemplified by the following reactions of ethene: **a** addition of hydrogen, steam, halogens and hydrogen halides, **b** oxidation by cold, dilute manganate(VII) to form the diol, and **c** oxidation by hot, concentrated manganate(VII) leading to the rupture of the carbon–carbon double bond;

12 describe and explain the mechanism of electrophilic addition in alkenes, using the addition of bromine to ethene as an example;

13 describe and explain the chemistry of arenes as exemplified by the following reactions of benzene and methylbenzene: **a** nitration, **b** substitution reactions with chlorine and with bromine, including the contrast with cyclohexene, and **c** oxidation of the side-chain to give a carboxylic acid;

14 describe and explain the mechanism of electrophilic substitution in arenes, using the mononitration of benzene as an example;

15 describe the effect of the delocalisation of electrons in arenes in such reactions;

16 predict, given the reaction conditions, whether halogenation will occur in the side-chain or the aromatic nucleus in arenes;

17 state the positions of substitution in methylbenzene;

18 discuss the use of alkanes and arenes in fuels, the occurrence of alkenes in living organisms and the uses of a variety of products from alkenes, such as plastics.

Sources of hydrocarbons

The fossil deposits of crude oil and natural gas have been the primary sources of alkanes throughout the twentieth century. Much of the wealth of the industrialised world can be ascribed to this exploitation of a natural resource. The vast majority of these deposits have been used to provide fuel for heating, electricity generation and transport. Smaller, but significant, proportions have been used to produce lubricants and to provide a source of hydrocarbons for the chemical process industry. In the UK, the chemical and petrochemical industries are by far the biggest contributors towards a positive balance in the value of manufacturing trade with the rest of the world. The UK chemical industry employs approximately 5% of the work force and produces about 9% of total industrial output. More than 41% of its sales are exports. *Figure 2.1* shows just how dependent the UK is on its chemical industry for the size of manufacturing exports.

Crude oil is a complex mixture of hydrocarbons. The composition of oil from different places varies considerably (*figure 2.2*). Three main series of hydrocarbons are present: aromatics, cycloalkanes and alkanes. At a given boiling point, the densities of these decrease in the order aromatic > cycloalkanes > alkanes. This provides a method for comparing the compositions of different oils.

A primary fractional distillation column is designed to separate crude oil into the following fractions: refinery gases, gasoline, kerosine, gas (diesel) oil and residue. The refinery gases consist of simple alkanes containing up to four carbon atoms. They are used as fuels or for building other molecules. Gasoline (petrol) contains alkanes with five to ten carbon atoms and is used as a fuel. Part of this fraction, naphtha, is used to make other chemicals. Naphtha is the fraction of crude oil which is the most important source of chemicals for the chemical process industry. Other fractions and natural gas are of lesser importance. Kerosine is used in aviation fuels and for domestic heating. Gas (diesel) oil is used as a vehicle fuel. The residue is used to make lubricating oils and waxes, and is also used to produce bitumen. Bitumen mixed with crushed stone is the tarmac used to surface roads. *Figure 2.3* shows a modern petrochemical plant.

After primary distillation, the different hydrocarbon fractions are treated in a variety of different ways. These include processes such as vacuum distillation (to separate out less volatile components such as arenes), desulphurisation (to remove sulphur) and cracking (to produce more gasoline and alkenes). There is insufficient gasoline fraction from

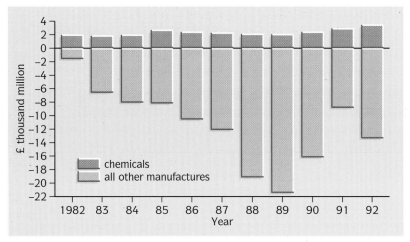

● **Figure 2.1** The UK balance of trade in chemicals compared with that in all other manufactures, 1982–92.

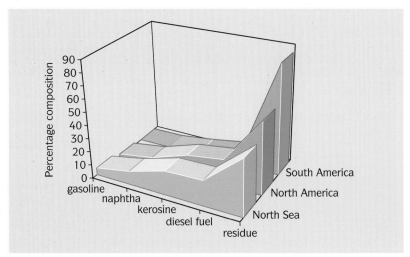

● **Figure 2.2** Breakdown of compositions of oils by oil fractions. North Sea oil contains a higher proportion of the gasoline and naphtha fractions than oils from North or South America.

● **Figure 2.3** A modern petrochemical plant. Pipes and fractional distillation columns dominate the skyline.

the primary distillation to satisfy the demand for petrol, so higher boiling fractions are cracked to produce more gasoline. Modern petrol engines require higher proportions of branched-chain alkanes, cycloalkanes and arenes to run well. These are produced by re-forming and isomerisation. The alkenes from cracking provide a very important feedstock to the chemical industry for making a wide range of products (page 86).

Cracking involves heating the oil fraction with a catalyst. Under these conditions, high-molecular-mass alkanes are broken down into low-molecular-mass alkanes as well as alkenes. Both C–C and C–H bonds are broken in the process. As the bond-breaking is a random process, a variety of products, including hydrogen, are possible and some of the intermediates can react to produce branched-chain alkane isomers. For example, a possible reaction equation for decane is:

$$CH_3CH_2CH_2CH_2CH_2CH_2CH_2CH_2CH_2CH_3$$
decane

$$\longrightarrow CH_3CH_2CH = CH_2 \quad + \quad H_3C-\overset{\overset{\displaystyle H}{|}}{\underset{\underset{\displaystyle CH_3}{|}}{C}}-CH_2CH_2CH_3$$
but-1-ene   2-methylpentane

SAQ 2.1

Write balanced equations showing the structural formulae for all the possible products formed on cracking pentane.

In the catalytic cracker *(figure 2.4)* the hot, vaporised oil fraction and the catalyst behave as a fluid. The seething mixture is called a **fluidised bed**. Some of the hydrocarbon mixture is broken down to carbon, which blocks the pores of the catalyst. The fluidised bed of the catalyst is pumped into a regeneration chamber, where the carbon coke is burnt off in air at a high temperature, allowing the catalyst to be recycled.

Re-forming and isomerisation provide two routes to increasing the supply of branched-chain alkanes. **Re-forming** involves the conversion of alkanes to cycloalkanes, or of cycloalkanes to arenes. Re-forming reactions are catalysed by bimetallic catalysts. For example, a cluster of platinum and rhenium atoms is very effective at

● *Figure 2.4* A catalytic cracker occupies the bulk of the central part of this photograph.

dehydrogenating methylcyclohexane to methylbenzene:

$$\langle\text{hexagon}\rangle-CH_3 \longrightarrow \langle\text{benzene}\rangle-CH_3 \; + \; 3H_2$$

A catalyst containing clusters of platinum and iridium atoms enables conversion of straight-chain alkanes to arenes:

$$CH_3CH_2CH_2CH_2CH_2CH_3 \longrightarrow \langle\text{benzene}\rangle \; + \; 4H_2$$

These metal clusters are between 1 and 5 nm in diameter and are deposited on an inert support such as aluminium oxide. The rhenium and iridium help prevent the build-up of carbon deposits, which reduce the activity of the catalysts.

Isomerisation involves heating the straight-chain isomers in the presence of a platinum catalyst:

$$CH_3CH_2CH_2CH_2CH_2CH_3 \longrightarrow H_3C-\overset{\overset{\displaystyle CH_3}{|}}{\underset{\underset{\displaystyle CH_3}{|}}{C}}-CH_2CH_3$$

The problems with using petrol

The petrol engine gives rise to a number of pollutants. The combustion of petrol as a motor fuel contributes significantly to the increase in carbon dioxide in the atmosphere. This increase in carbon dioxide is the main cause of global warming by the 'greenhouse effect'. Whilst global warming is a long-term concern, the atmospheric abundance of carbon dioxide is about 0.035%, which is well below the level at which it is harmful to people (about 1%). A reduction in emissions of carbon dioxide can only be brought about by a decrease in the use of fossil fuels such as petrol. This could be achieved by cutting down dramatically on the use of motorised transport, or by finding an alternative to fossil fuels that does not contain carbon. Many scientists now believe that hydrogen is the only pollution-free alternative.

Of more immediate concern are the much more harmful pollutants carbon monoxide, nitrogen(II) oxide and hydrocarbons. Carbon monoxide and hydrocarbons are emitted by the incomplete combustion of petrol in engines. Nitrogen(II) oxide is formed in engines by the reaction of nitrogen and oxygen at high temperature:

$$N_2(g) + O_2(g) \longrightarrow 2NO(g)$$

Carbon monoxide combines with haemoglobin in the blood, preventing the transport of oxygen. The levels of carbon monoxide in heavy traffic are sufficient to affect the brain and may contribute to accidents. Nitrogen(II) oxide is rapidly oxidised to nitrogen(IV) oxide in air:

$$2NO(g) + O_2(g) \longrightarrow 2NO_2(g)$$

Nitrogen(IV) oxide is an irritant to the respiratory system and the eyes. It is likely to increase breathing difficulties in asthmatics. Like sulphur dioxide, it is a major cause of acid rain and has been found to harm trees.

The quantities of unburnt hydrocarbons are increased by the evaporation of fuel. Fumes from the evaporation of fuel are usually most concentrated on petrol station forecourts and inside the passenger compartment of a car. These fumes contain aromatic hydrocarbons such as benzene. This is of particular concern, as benzene has been implicated as a cause of leukaemia in young children.

Unfortunately the problems do not end here: the combination of these exhaust emissions can lead to the formation of **photochemical smog** *(figure 2.5)*. This is caused by a complex series of photochemical reactions. Such reactions are initiated by light

● *Figure 2.5* Photochemical smog over Denver, Colorado, USA.

and involve breaking bonds to form free radicals. These reactions take place in high levels of exhaust emissions, which become trapped in the air above a city in certain weather conditions. Ultraviolet radiation in the sunlight is absorbed by nitrogen(IV) oxide, which breaks down to nitrogen(II) oxide and oxygen atoms:

$$NO_2(g) \xrightarrow{hf} NO(g) + O(g)$$

The oxygen atoms combine with oxygen molecules to form low-level ozone:

$$O_2(g) + O(g) \longrightarrow O_3(g)$$

The mixture of ozone, oxides of nitrogen, hydrocarbons and carbon monoxide produces a wide range of products (such as peroxyacetyl nitrate, PAN) by many different reactions. Many of these products are irritating to the eyes, nose and throat. Ozone and PAN are particularly irritating *(figure 2.6)*. Both may be contributing to the increase in asthma attacks during the summer months in the UK.

You can find out more about atmospheric pollutants in the *Environmental Chemistry* book in this series.

Reducing harmful emissions

Whilst improved engineering and maintenance help to keep emissions to relatively low levels, they have only a small effect on overall levels of emissions. Catalytic converters can help by reducing

● *Figure 2.6* A cyclist wearing an air filter as a protection against pollution. A filter such as this might contain an activated form of carbon, which will absorb pollutant gases.

these emission levels further, but to be properly effective, catalytic converters must be capable of removing carbon monoxide, oxides of nitrogen and hydrocarbons. Such converters are called three-way catalytic converters (*figure 2.7*). Oxides of nitrogen are catalytically reduced by carbon monoxide:

$$2NO(g) + 2CO(g) \longrightarrow N_2(g) + 2CO_2(g)$$

Carbon monoxide and hydrocarbons (for example, octane) are oxidised:

$$2CO(g) + O_2(g) \longrightarrow 2CO_2(g)$$
$$2C_8H_{18}(g) + 25O_2(g) \longrightarrow 16CO_2(g) + 18H_2O(g)$$

● *Figure 2.7* Concerns about the adverse effects of photochemical smog have led to the introduction of legislation in many countries to control the levels of exhaust emissions. One way of controlling emissions is to fit vehicles with three-way catalytic converters, such as the one shown here.

Diesel engines also produce harmful emissions, such as polyaromatic hydrocarbons. These are very undesirable emissions as they, like benzene, may cause cancer. However, diesel engines can now be fitted with a catalytic converter.

Despite all these measures to reduce emissions, the most effective measure is to reduce the use of hydrocarbons as a fuel – either by using other methods of propulsion (for example electric motors) or, best of all, by reducing the use of motor vehicles.

The properties of alkanes

The atoms in alkanes are held together by σ orbitals. A **σ orbital** lies predominantly along the axis between two nuclei. It may be regarded as being formed by the overlap of two atomic s orbitals. The two electrons in the orbital attract both nuclei, binding them together in a **σ bond**. The geometry of alkane molecules is based on the tetrahedral arrangement of four covalent σ bonds round each carbon atom. The σ bonds lie between a carbon atom and either a hydrogen atom or another carbon atom. All bond angles are 109.5°. The molecules can rotate freely about each carbon–carbon single bond. This freedom to rotate allows a great degree of flexibility to alkane chains (page 7). The σ bonds in ethane are shown in *figure 2.8*.

Alkanes are remarkably inert compounds. Although they make excellent fuels, their oxidation

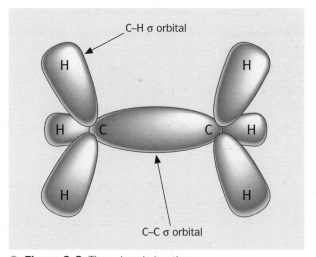

● *Figure 2.8* The σ bonds in ethane.

Bond	Energy/kJ mol^{-1}
C–H	413
O–H	464
C–C	347
C=C	612
C=O	805
C–O	336
O=O	498

● **Table 2.1** Bond energies

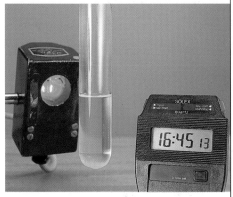

● **Figure 2.9** The reaction of bromine with hexane in ultraviolet light.

reactions have high activation energies and require a significant input of energy before ignition. This energy input may come from a spark, as in the internal combustion engine, or from the match used to light a Bunsen burner. One of the reasons for this inertness is the relatively high bond energies of C–H and C–C bonds.

SAQ 2.2

Butane is widely used as a fuel in camping stoves.

a Write a balanced equation for the combustion of one mole of butane.

b With reference to *table 2.1*, calculate the energy required to break the C–C and C–H bonds in butane and the O=O bond in oxygen.

c Calculate the energy released on forming the C=O bonds in carbon dioxide and the O–H bonds in water.

d Use your balanced equation, the energy input calculated in **b** and the energy output in **c** to calculate the enthalpy change of combustion of butane.

e Explain why butane requires a lighted match to start it burning, even though it has a large, exothermic enthalpy change of combustion.

A second, very important, reason for the inertness of alkanes arises from their lack of polarity. As carbon and hydrogen have very similar electronegativities, alkanes are non-polar molecules. Consequently, alkanes are not readily attacked by common chemical reagents. Most reagents that you have met are highly polar compounds. For example, water, acids, alkalis and many oxidising and reducing agents are polar, and they usually initiate reactions by their attraction to polar groups in other compounds. Such polar reagents do not react with alkanes.

Some non-polar reagents will react with alkanes. The most important of these are the halogens, which, in the presence of ultraviolet light, will *substitute* hydrogen atoms in the alkane with halogen atoms. For example, when chlorine is mixed with methane and exposed to sunlight, chloromethane is formed and hydrogen chloride gas is evolved:

$$CH_4(g) + Cl_2(g) \longrightarrow CH_3Cl(g) + HCl(g)$$

Because the reaction requires ultraviolet light it is a photochemical reaction.

Further substitution is possible, producing in turn dichloromethane, trichloromethane and tetrachloromethane. Other halogens such as bromine produce similar substitution products. With hexane, for example, bromine produces bromohexane (*figure 2.9*):

$$C_6H_{14}(l) + Br_2(l) \longrightarrow C_6H_{13}Br(l) + HBr(g)$$

The substitution mechanism

The overall equation for a reaction gives no clue as to the stages involved between reactants and products. The sequence of stages is known as the **mechanism** of a reaction. For example, the energy of ultraviolet light is sufficient to break the Cl–Cl bond. Absorption of light energy causing a bond to break is known as **photodissociation**. Homolytic fission (page 16) occurs and two chlorine atoms are formed, each having seven electrons in their outer shell. The chlorine atoms each have one unpaired electron and are thus free radicals (page 16). Free radicals react very rapidly with other molecules or chemical species. As the homolytic fission of a chlorine molecule must occur before any chloromethane can be formed, it is known as the **initiation step**.

$$Cl \frown Cl \text{ (g)} \xrightarrow{hf} Cl \bullet \text{ (g)} + Cl \bullet \text{ (g)}$$

The half-headed curly arrow shows the movement of one electron.

The reaction of a chlorine atom with a methane molecule produces hydrogen chloride and a $CH_3\bullet$ free radical. The dot indicates the unpaired electron. The carbon atom in this $CH_3\bullet$ fragment also has seven electrons in its outer shell. A methyl free radical can react with a chlorine molecule to produce chloromethane and a new chlorine atom:

$$Cl\bullet \text{ (g)} + H \frown CH_3 \text{ (g)} \longrightarrow Cl—H \text{ (g)} + CH_3\bullet \text{ (g)}$$

$$CH_3\bullet \text{ (g)} + Cl \frown Cl \text{ (g)} \longrightarrow CH_3Cl \text{ (g)} + Cl\bullet \text{ (g)}$$

These two steps enable the reaction to continue. In the first step, a chlorine free radical is used up. The second step releases a new chlorine free radical, which can allow repetition of the first step. The reaction will continue for as long as there is a supply of methane molecules and undissociated chlorine molecules. The two steps constitute a **chain reaction** and are known as the **propagation steps** of the reaction.

The reaction to form chloromethane and hydrogen chloride ceases when the supply of reagents is depleted. There is a variety of possible termination steps. These include recombination of chlorine free radicals to form chlorine molecules.

Alternatively, two methyl free radicals can combine to form an ethane molecule:

$$Cl\bullet \text{ (g)} + Cl\bullet \text{ (g)} \longrightarrow Cl_2 \text{ (g)}$$

$$CH_3\bullet \text{ (g)} + CH_3\bullet \text{ (g)} \longrightarrow CH_3CH_3 \text{ (g)}$$

These, or any other, termination steps will remove free radicals and disrupt the propagation steps, thus stopping the chain reaction.

The four steps involved in the formation of chloromethane and hydrogen chloride from methane and chlorine constitute the mechanism of this reaction. As the reaction is a substitution involving free radicals, it is known as a **free-radical substitution**.

SAQ 2.3

a Which of the following reagents are likely to produce free radicals in ultraviolet light?
$HCl(aq)$, $Br_2(l)$, $NaOH(aq)$, $Cl_2(g)$, $KMnO_4(aq)$.

b Write balanced equations for the reactions of butane with those reagents that produce free radicals.

Alkenes

A number of biologically important molecules are alkenes. Many of these are based on the simple diene, isoprene (2-methylbuta-1,3-diene):

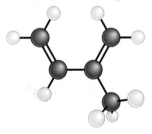

Some trees can be tapped for their latex or natural rubber (*figure 2.10*). Latex is a polymer of isoprene. The natural oil, limonene, present in the rind of oranges and lemons is derived from two isoprene units:

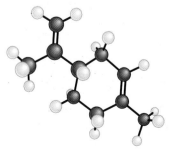

● **Figure 2.10** Scraping the bark off a rubber tree in this way causes the liquid rubber to accumulate at one point, where it can be collected.

Carotene, responsible for the orange colouring in carrots, is based on eight isoprene units:

In the intestine, carotene is broken down into vitamin A, which is based on four isoprene units:

Vitamin A is an essential micronutrient that influences growth and helps prevent night-blindness in animals. Alkenes are used to make many chemicals that feature prominently in modern life. Some examples of these chemicals are shown in *figure 2.11*.

Bonding in alkenes: σ and π bonds.

Simple alkenes are hydrocarbons that contain one carbon–carbon double bond. The simplest alkene is ethene, $CH_2=CH_2$. The general formula of the homologous series of alkenes is C_nH_{2n}.

SAQ 2.4

Draw a dot-and-cross diagram for ethene. Predict the shape of the molecule and give estimates of the bond angles.

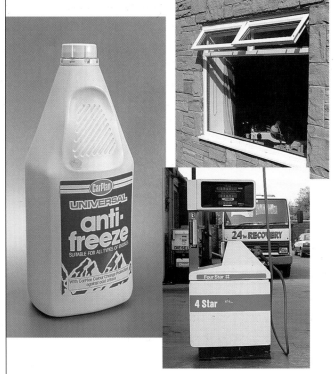

● **Figure 2.11** A range of products produced from alkenes, including poly(chloroethene) window frames, ethane-1,2-diol (used in antifreeze) and 1,2-dibromoethane and tetraethyl lead (used as additives in leaded petrol).

Electrons in molecules occupy σ and π molecular orbitals. A π orbital (or π bond) lies predominantly in two lobes, one on each side of a σ bond. Overlap of two atomic p orbitals produces a π molecular orbital or π **bond**. To ensure maximum overlap, ethene must be a planar molecule. A single covalent bond, such as C–C or C–H, consists of a σ bond. Double bonds such as C=C consist of one σ bond and one π bond.

overlap of p orbitals produces
π molecular orbitals

Compounds which contain π bonds, such as ethene, are called unsaturated compounds. The term **unsaturated** indicates that the compound will combine by *addition* reactions with hydrogen or other chemicals, losing its multiple bonds.

Saturated compounds contain only *single* carbon–carbon bonds. The terms 'saturated' and 'unsaturated' are often used in connection with oils and fats. The molecules in vegetable oils contain several double bonds – they are described as **polyunsaturated**. In hard margarine, hydrogen has been added to these double bonds so the margarine is now saturated. However, several of the fatty acids which are essential to our diet are polyunsaturated and so, to ensure that these fatty acids are retained, much modern margarine is only partially saturated.

Cis–trans isomerism

Many alkenes exhibit *cis–trans* isomerism; we shall consider an example. Natural rubber is a polymer of 2-methylbuta-1,3-diene (or isoprene, page 25). The repeating unit contains a carbon–carbon double bond. All the links between the isoprene units are on the same side of this double bond. This arrangement is described as the *cis* isomer:

$$-\underset{H_3C}{\overset{H_2}{C}}\!\!\diagdown\!\!\underset{}{C}\!\!=\!\!\underset{H}{\overset{}{C}}\!\!\diagup\!\!\underset{H_3C}{\overset{H_2}{C}}\!\!-\!\!\underset{}{\overset{H_2}{C}}\!\!\diagdown\!\!\underset{}{C}\!\!=\!\!\underset{H}{\overset{}{C}}\!\!\diagup\!\!\underset{H_3C}{\overset{H_2}{C}}\!\!-\!\!\underset{}{\overset{H_2}{C}}\!\!\diagdown\!\!\underset{}{C}\!\!=\!\!\underset{H}{\overset{}{C}}\!\!\diagup\!\!\overset{H_2}{C}-$$

cis-poly(2-methylbuta-1,3-diene) natural rubber

Natural rubber is the familiar material used for balloons, rubber gloves and condoms.

Another possible arrangement has the links between each 2-methylbuta-1,3-diene unit on alternate sides of the double bond. As they lie across the double bond, this is the *trans* isomer. It is found naturally as gutta-percha, which is a grey, inelastic, horny material obtained from the percha tree in Malaysia. It is used in the manufacture of golf balls.

trans-poly(2-methylbuta-1,3-diene) gutta-percha

Both *cis*- and *trans*-2-methylbuta-1,3-diene can be manufactured from 2-methylbuta-1,3-diene using appropriate Ziegler–Natta catalysts. Such catalysts were developed by the German chemist Karl Ziegler and the Italian chemist Giulio Natta, and are based on triethylaluminium and titanium(IV) chloride. Ziegler and Natta made a

substantial contribution to the development of polymers and were jointly awarded the Nobel prize for chemistry in 1963.

Cis–trans isomerism is frequently encountered in alkenes, and arises because rotation about a double bond cannot occur unless the π bond is broken. In addition to a double bond, the molecule must have two identical groups, one on each of the two carbon atoms involved in the double bond. The other two groups must be different to this identical pair. But-2-ene is the simplest alkene to show *cis–trans* isomerism:

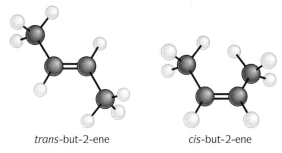

trans-but-2-ene cis-but-2-ene

In the *cis* isomer, two methyl groups are on the same side of the double bond; in the *trans* isomer they are on opposite sides.

SAQ 2.5

Consider the following:

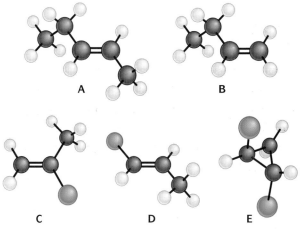

a Which, apart from **A**, can exist as *cis–trans* isomers?

b Draw and name the structural formulae for the pair of *cis–trans* isomers for **A**.

Addition to the double bond

Addition reactions are characteristic of an alkene (page 15). In this chapter we shall look at the reactions of some small molecules to alkenes. The addition of an alkene to itself (addition polymerisation) is discussed in chapter 8 (page 86).

■ *Addition of hydrogen*

This converts the unsaturated alkene to a saturated alkane. Hydrogen gas and a gaseous alkene are passed over a finely divided nickel catalyst supported on an inert material. The equation for the addition of hydrogen to cyclohexene is:

Another example is the manufacture of margarine from vegetable oil at a temperature of about 450 K and a hydrogen pressure of up to 1000 kPa (*figure 2.12*).

■ *Addition of water*

This is a route to making alcohols. Industrially, steam and a gaseous alkene are passed over a solid catalyst; usually a temperature of 600 K and a pressure of 6 MPa are used in the presence of a phosphoric acid catalyst. For example, ethene and steam produce ethanol:

$$CH_2=CH_2(g) + H_2O(g)$$
$$\longrightarrow CH_3CH_2OH(l)$$

● **Figure 2.12** A hydrogenation vessel for making margarine.

● **Figure 2.13** The reaction of ethene with a solution of bromine.

■ *Addition of halogens*

When an alkene such as propene is bubbled through a solution of bromine at room temperature, the bromine solution is rapidly decolourised from its characteristic orange colour (*figure 2.13*). Unlike free-radical substitution on an alkane, this reaction does not require ultraviolet light and will occur in total darkness. The bromine joins to the propene to form 1,2-dibromopropane:

$$CH_3CH=CH_2 + Br_2 \longrightarrow CH_3CHBrCH_2Br$$

Chlorine and iodine produce similar addition products. Fluorine is too powerful an oxidant and tends to ignite hydrocarbons!

■ *Addition of hydrogen halides*

Hydrogen halides also add readily to alkenes. Ethene produces chloroethane on bubbling through concentrated aqueous hydrochloric acid at room temperature:

$$CH_2=CH_2(g) + HCl(aq) \longrightarrow CH_3CH_2Cl(l)$$

The reactivity of the hydrogen halides increases from HF to HI, following the order of decreasing bond energy. Hydrogen fluoride will react with an alkene only under pressure. Alkenes such as propene can give rise to two different products:

$$CH_3CH=CH_2 + HBr \longrightarrow CH_3CHBrCH_3 \text{ or } CH_3CH_2CH_2Br$$

The normal product is 2-bromopropane, $CH_3CHBrCH_3$. This is formed by an electrophilic substitution mechanism (page 34). As the intermediate in this mechanism involves a carbocation, the product is dependent on the relative stabilities of the two possible carbocations. The hydrogen from the hydrogen bromide is the electrophilic end of the molecule, and it attacks the propene to form

H
⊕|
  C
H ⟋ ⟍ CH₂CH₃
primary carbocation

or

H
⊕|
  C
H₃C ⟋ ⟍ CH₃
secondary carbocation

The secondary carbocation is stabilised by the inductive effects (page 17) of two alkyl groups; the primary carbocation is stabilised by the inductive effect of only one alkyl group. Hence the secondary carbocation is more stable than the primary carbocation, and for this reason it is preferred. Therefore the bromine from the hydrogen bromide will join at the 2 position on the carbocation. One way to remember which product is formed is to use **Markovnikov's rule:** The hydrogen atom joins the carbon in the double bond with more hydrogen atoms already attached.

The alternative product 1-bromopropane, $CH_3CH_2CH_2Br$, is formed when the reaction mixture is exposed to ultraviolet light. This suggests that a different mechanism takes place, involving free radicals.

SAQ 2.6

Draw structures for the products formed when cyclohexene reacts with **a** iodine, **b** hydrogen iodide and **c** water (as steam). In each case, write down the conditions required for the reaction to occur.

Oxidation of alkenes

Mild conditions

Alkenes decolourise acidified potassium manganate(VII) on warming *(figure 2.14)*. The alkene is oxidised to a diol. Two alcohol functional groups (–OH) become attached to the carbon atoms on either side of the π bond. The potassium

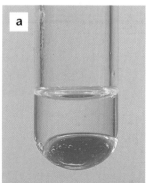 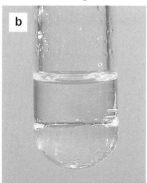

● **Figure 2.14** The reaction of cyclohexene with acidified potassium manganate(VII).
a Before reaction.
b After reaction.

manganate(VII) acts as an oxidising agent and provides one of the oxygen atoms; the other oxygen atom and the hydrogen atoms come from a water molecule. In organic reactions, the oxygen from an oxidising agent is often represented by [O]. This enables a simpler equation to be written, for example:

$$CH_2=CH_2 + [O] + H_2O \longrightarrow CH_2OHCH_2OH$$

The product from the oxidation of ethene in this way is ethane-1,2-diol. Industrially, this reaction is carried out using oxygen from the air with a silver catalyst, followed by treatment with water.

SAQ 2.7

Draw structural formulae for **a** the reaction of but-2-ene with hydrogen bromide and **b** the product obtained by warming propene with acidified potassium manganate(VII).

More vigorous conditions

If an alkene is refluxed with hot concentrated potassium manganate(VII), the double bond is broken to produce two organic products. Identification of the two products enables the position of the double bond in the alkene to be determined. For example, the treatment of pent-2-ene under these conditions produces ethanoic acid and propanoic acid:

$$CH_3CH=CHCH_2CH_3(l) + 4[O]$$
$$\longrightarrow CH_3COOH(aq) + CH_3CH_2COOH(aq)$$

This may be seen by breaking the pent-2-ene at the double bond and replacing it with a C=O double bond on each carbon. Two aldehydes would result, which would be further oxidised to the two carboxylic acids in the equation.

SAQ 2.8

a Treatment of 2-methylbut-2-ene by refluxing with concentrated acidified potassium manganate(VII) produces a ketone and a carboxylic acid. Write a balanced equation for this oxidation, using structural formulae.

b On refluxing with concentrated acidified potassium manganate(VII), an alkene produces propanone only. Draw a structural formula for the alkene and write a balanced equation for the reaction.

Test	Observation if an alkene is present
shake alkene with bromine water	orange bromine water is decolourised
shake alkene with acidified aqueous potassium manganate(VII)	purple potassium manganate(VII) is decolourised

● **Table 2.2** Simple tests for alkenes

The mechanism of addition

Although bromine and ethene are non-polar reagents, the bromine molecule becomes polarised when close to a region of negative charge such as the ethene π bond. The π bond then breaks, with its electron-pair forming a new covalent bond to the bromine atom, which carries a partial, positive charge. At the same time, the bromine molecule undergoes heterolytic fission (page 16). Heterolytic fission involves both electrons in the bond moving to the same atom. These changes produce a bromide ion and a positively charged carbon atom (a carbocation) in the ethene molecule (*figure 2.15*). Carbocations are highly reactive and the bromide ion rapidly forms a second carbon–bromine covalent bond to give 1,2-dibromoethane.

In this mechanism, the polarised bromine molecule has behaved as an electrophile. An **electrophile** is a reactant which is attracted to an electron-rich centre or atom, where it accepts a pair of electrons to form a new covalent bond. The reaction is an example of one which proceeds by an **electrophilic addition** mechanism.

● **Figure 2.15** The formation of a carbocation in the bromination of ethene.

SAQ 2.9

a Draw a dot-and-cross diagram of the carbocation formed in an electrophilic addition to ethene. How many electrons are there on the positively charged carbon atom? Explain how this atom completes its outer electron shell when it combines with a bromide ion.

b Suggest a mechanism for the addition of hydrogen chloride to ethene.

Arenes

The simplest arene is benzene. Benzene is added to unleaded petrol and is used to make many other chemicals, as shown in the pie chart (*figure 2.16*): 65% of benzene is used to make alkylbenzenes. These include ethylbenzene (used to make phenylethene, the monomer for poly(phenylethene), more commonly known as polystyrene); dodecylbenzene (which is used to make detergents) and 1-methylethylbenzene (cumene), used to make phenol and propanone. The benzene ring may be found in compounds as varied as medicines, dyes and explosives (*figure 2.17*). Cyclohexane, which is a starting material for making nylon, is also made from benzene. You will not use benzene in a school laboratory as it is believed to cause leukaemia.

Benzene is a planar hexagonal molecule. This structure has considerable chemical stability. Kekulé was first to suggest that benzene was a cyclic molecule with alternating single and double carbon–carbon bonds. Such a structure would have two different lengths for the carbon–carbon bonds. The single and double bonds may be placed in two

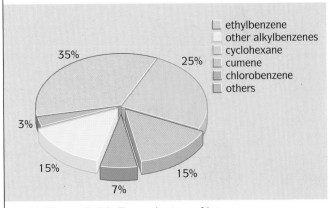

	ethylbenzene
	other alkylbenzenes
	cyclohexane
	cumene
	chlorobenzene
	others

● **Figure 2.16** The main uses of benzene.

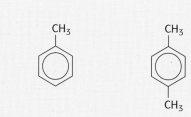

methylbenzene (toluene) and 1,4-dimethylbenzene (xylene) – additives which improve the performance of petrol

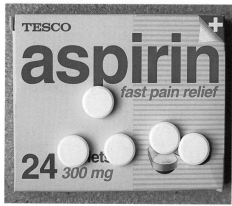

vanillin – present in oil of vanilla extracted from the pod of the vanilla orchid, and familiar as vanilla flavouring

aspirin – used as an analgesic (pain killer)

a diazo dye – used as colouring in paints and on fabrics

● *Figure 2.17*

alternative positions:

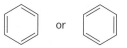

(It may help you to see these as alternative positions if you imagine that you are standing on the carbon atom at 12 o'clock: one structure will have the double bond on your left, the other has the double bond on the right.)

The Kekulé structure for benzene would be expected to show the typical addition reactions of an alkene. However, benzene undergoes addition reactions far less easily than a typical alkene. For example, an alkene such as cyclohexene will rapidly decolourise aqueous bromine in the dark. Bromine must be dissolved in boiling benzene and exposed to ultraviolet light before addition occurs.

Also, the carbon–carbon bond lengths in benzene molecules are all identical, with lengths intermediate between those of single and double bonds *(table 2.3)*.

The current model of the bonding in benzene accounts for these observations. Each carbon atom contributes one electron to a π bond. However, the π bonds formed do not lie between pairs of carbon atoms as in an alkene: the π bonds spread over all six carbon atoms. The electrons occupy three delocalised π orbitals. They are

Bond	Bond length/nm
C–C	0.154
C=C	0.134
benzene C–C	0.139

● *Table 2.3* Carbon–carbon bond lengths

said to be **delocalised** as they are not localised between adjacent pairs of carbon atoms but are spread over all six. (An alkene π bond *is* localised between a pair of carbon atoms.) The π molecular orbitals are formed by overlap of carbon p atomic orbitals. To achieve maximum overlap, the benzene molecule must be planar. One of the delocalised π molecular orbitals is shown below:

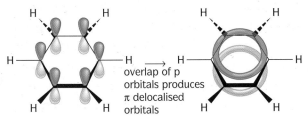

overlap of p orbitals produces π delocalised orbitals

This model produces six C–C bonds of the same length, as observed. The planar shape is clearly seen in a space-filling molecular model of benzene:

The reluctance of benzene to undergo addition reactions is due to the additional energetic stability that the delocalised system gives it. A measure of this additional stability can be seen by considering the enthalpy changes for the addition of chlorine to cyclohexene and to benzene.

Addition reaction with chlorine

Benzene has been used to manufacture the insecticide Lindane. Lindane is an isomer of 1,2,3,4,5,6-hexachlorocyclohexane. Three moles of chlorine will react with one mole of benzene in an addition reaction:

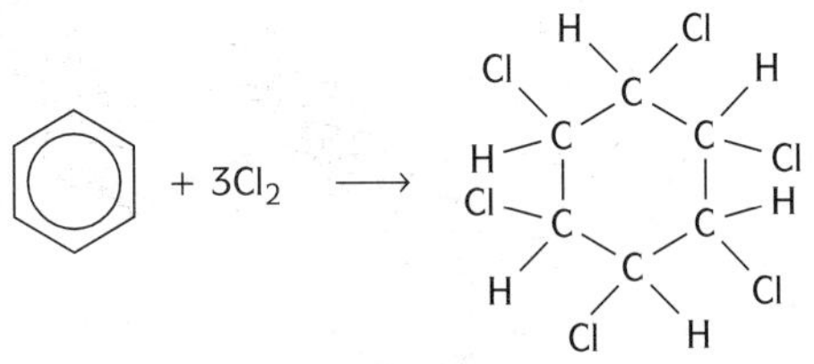

The conditions required for the addition of chlorine to benzene are much more vigorous than those required for the addition of chlorine to a simple alkene. Chlorine will participate in addition on mixing with a gaseous alkene or bubbling through a liquid alkene without heat or a catalyst. The reaction will also take place in the dark. Benzene, however, requires the chlorine to be bubbled through the boiling liquid in ultraviolet light.

SAQ 2.10

a What does the use of ultraviolet light suggest about the nature of the attacking species in the addition of chlorine to benzene?

b How does your suggestion compare to the attacking species in the addition of chlorine to an alkene?

Benzene requires more vigorous reaction conditions because of the extra chemical stability of the delocalised electron system. Extra energy is required to overcome this stability. A comparison of the enthalpy changes for the reactions of chlorine with benzene or cyclohexene provides a measure of this extra energetic stability. The equations and enthalpy changes are as follows:

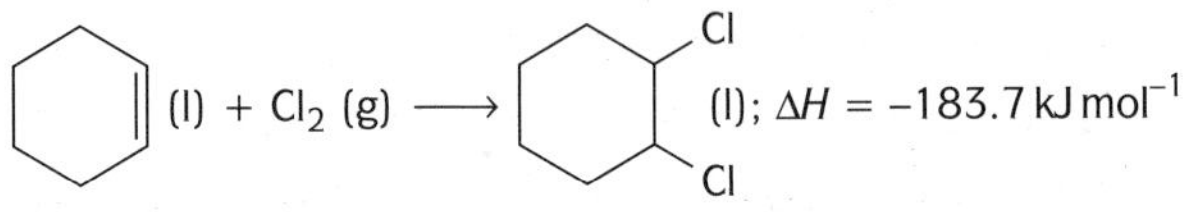

$$\text{(l)} + Cl_2 \text{ (g)} \longrightarrow \text{(l)}; \Delta H = -183.7 \text{ kJ mol}^{-1}$$

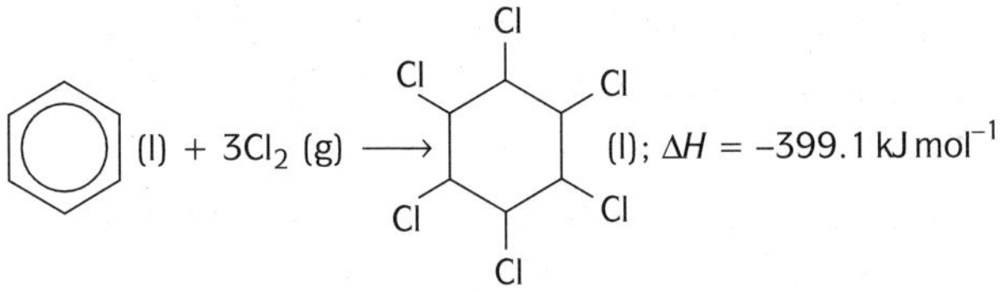

$$\text{(l)} + 3Cl_2 \text{ (g)} \longrightarrow \text{(l)}; \Delta H = -399.1 \text{ kJ mol}^{-1}$$

If benzene had the Kekulé (or cyclohexatriene) structure with alternating single and double bonds, it would be reasonable to suppose that the enthalpy change on reacting benzene with three moles of chlorine would be three times that of the addition of one mole of chlorine to a mole of cyclohexene:

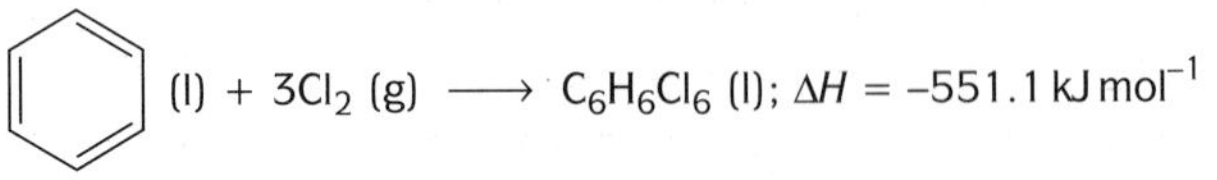

$$\text{(l)} + 3Cl_2 \text{ (g)} \longrightarrow C_6H_6Cl_6 \text{ (l)}; \Delta H = -551.1 \text{ kJ mol}^{-1}$$

However, this is 152 kJ mol^{-1} more exothermic than the experimentally derived value. The extra energy is needed to overcome the delocalisation of the π electron bonds. This energy is sometimes referred to as the **stabilisation** (or delocalisation) energy of benzene.

Substitution reactions

As you have seen, breaking the delocalised π electron system on benzene requires a considerable input of energy. Arenes such as benzene exhibit many reactions in which the delocalised system is retained. The majority of these are substitution reactions. Groups which may directly replace a hydrogen atom on a benzene ring include halogen atoms, nitro ($-NO_2$) groups, alkyl groups and sulphonic acid ($-SO_2OH$) groups.

The formation of nitroarenes

The explosive trinitrotoluene (TNT) is made by substituting nitro groups, $-NO_2$, for hydrogen atoms on the benzene ring of methylbenzene (toluene). It is explosive because the nitro groups bring six oxygen atoms into close proximity to the carbon atoms of the benzene ring. When detonated, the compression pushes these atoms closer together, causing rapid formation of carbon dioxide and water vapour, and leaving the nitrogen atoms to join together as nitrogen molecules. The explosion is caused by the very large and rapid increase in volume as the solid TNT is converted to gases. (There is not sufficient oxygen to convert all the carbon to carbon dioxide, so carbon is also formed and is seen as black smoke.)

In addition to its use in explosives, the nitro group is a versatile and useful group in the preparation of drugs and dyestuffs.

The **method for making nitrobenzene** is quite sophisticated, and **safety precautions** must be taken. Until the hazardous nature of benzene was fully appreciated and its use in schools and colleges was banned, the preparation of nitrobenzene was a routine practical in A level chemistry. Nitrobenzene is also harmful, and its preparation from benzene would require the use of an efficient fume cupboard. You may have the chance to nitrate a substituted benzene such as the much less harmful methyl benzoate. Both benzene and methyl benzoate require the use of **nitrating**

mixture. This is a mixture containing equal volumes of concentrated nitric acid and concentrated sulphuric acid. Care needs to be taken in its preparation and use as it is highly corrosive. The two acids are mixed by adding the concentrated sulphuric acid slowly, with cooling, to the concentrated nitric acid. As the nitrating mixture is cooled, it is then mixed with benzene in a flask fitted with a condenser for reflux. The reaction mixture is heated gently under reflux at a temperature of about 50–55 °C. Careful temperature control is needed to minimise the quantity of dinitrobenzene formed. The impure nitrobenzene is obtained by pouring the cooled reaction mixture into cold water *(figure 2.18)*. The product is an almond-smelling, yellow oil. It may be purified by washing it with aqueous sodium carbonate in a separating funnel, drying the washed oil over an anhydrous salt such as calcium chloride, and then distilling the oil. The reaction equation is:

This is a substitution in which a hydrogen atom has been replaced by the nitro group.

Methylbenzene may also be nitrated using

● *Figure 2.18* Nitrobenzene separates as an oil when the reaction mixture is poured into water.

nitrating mixture. Monosubstitution might give rise to three different products:

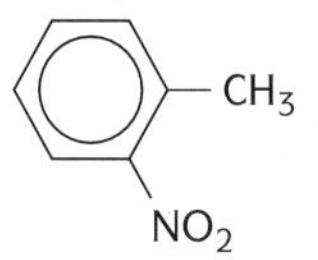

2-nitromethylbenzene

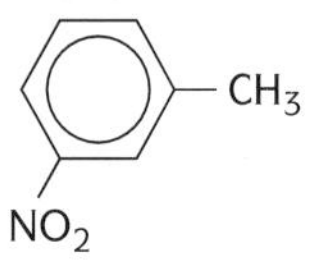

3-nitromethylbenzene

4-nitromethylbenzene

In practice, a mixture of 2-nitromethylbenzene and 4-nitromethylbenzene is produced. Whilst further nitration of methylbenzene is possible at higher temperatures to produce dinitromethylbenzenes, nitration to produce 2,4,6-trinitromethylbenzene requires special conditions.

SAQ 2.11

Draw the structural formulae of, and name all the dinitro-methylbenzenes that might be formed from methylbenzene. Indicate which of these you would expect to be formed.

The **mechanism of nitration** involves an electrophilic substitution. The function of the sulphuric acid in the nitrating mixture is to generate the attacking species from the nitric acid. (An attacking species may be a reactive molecule, a free radical or an ion.) The benzene ring has a high electron charge density associated with the delocalised π electrons. Hence an attacking reagent that is attracted by this negative charge is needed – an electrophile. An electrophile must be capable of forming a new covalent bond to carbon if it is to react successfully.

The electrophile produced in the nitrating mixture is the nitryl cation, NO_2^+:

$$H_2SO_4 + HNO_3 \longrightarrow NO_2^+ + HSO_4^- + H_2O$$

This nitryl cation is attracted by the delocalised π electrons:

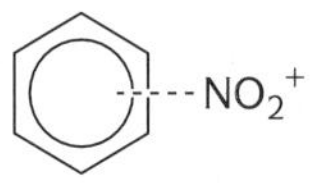

The dotted line represents the attraction between the nitryl cation and the delocalised π electrons. This is followed by a covalent bond forming to one of the carbon atoms in the benzene ring. This carbon atom is now saturated, so the delocalised electrons, together with the positive charge from the NO_2^+, are shared by the remaining five carbon atoms. Loss of a proton (H^+) produces the nitrobenzene product and restores the full, delocalised π-electron system:

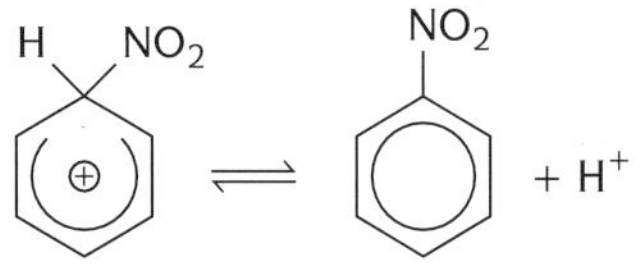

Thus in electrophilic substitution, the chemical stability of the benzene ring is retained.

When methylbenzene is nitrated, the electrophilic nitryl cation produces 2-nitromethylbenzene and 4-nitromethylbenzene. No 3-nitromethylbenzene is formed. This is because the positive inductive effect of the methyl group increases the electron charge density on the benzene ring at the 2, 4 and 6 positions. Hence nitration occurs preferentially in these positions.

Other groups on benzene may have a negative inductive effect, withdrawing electron charge from the 2, 4 and 6 positions. Substitution in the presence of such groups will occur at the 3 and 5 positions.

The formation of halogenoarenes

As well as undergoing an addition reaction with chlorine, benzene will also undergo an electrophilic substitution reaction with chlorine or bromine. For example, if chlorine is bubbled through benzene in the presence of a catalyst, chlorobenzene is formed at room temperature:

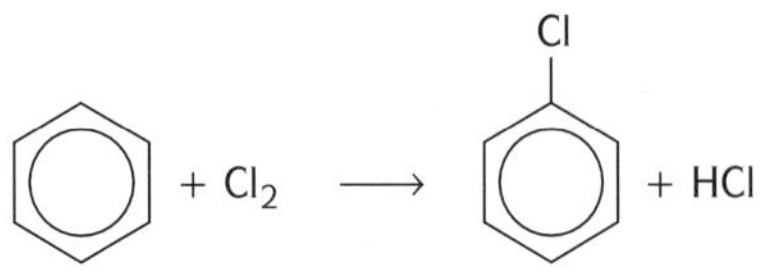

The catalyst is usually introduced as metallic iron. This reacts with the chlorine to produce iron(III) chloride. Like anhydrous aluminium chloride, this is a covalent chloride and is soluble in the benzene.

The effect of the iron(III) chloride is to polarise the chlorine molecule so that it behaves as an electrophile:

$$\overset{\delta+}{Cl} \text{---} \overset{\delta-}{Cl} \text{---} FeCl_3$$

The dotted lines show bonds breaking between chlorine atoms and forming between a chlorine atom and the iron(III) chloride. Anhydrous aluminium chloride may also be used as a catalyst.

Electrophilic substitution will also take place between methylbenzene and chlorine or bromine. Monosubstitution could give rise to three different products. For example, with bromine:

2-bromomethylbenzene

3-bromomethylbenzene

4-bromomethylbenzene

In practice, as with nitration, a mixture of 2-bromomethylbenzene and 4-bromomethylbenzene is produced. This is because the positive inductive effect of the methyl group increases the electron charge density on the benzene ring more strongly at the 2, 4 and 6 positions.

SAQ 2.12

a   Suggest the stages involved in the mechanism for substitution by chlorine on benzene.

b   Draw structural formulae for the monosubstituted products formed when chlorine reacts with methyl-benzene at room temperature (i) in the presence of an iron(III) chloride catalyst and (ii) in ultraviolet light at room temperature.

The formation of alkylbenzenes

Alkylbenzenes are made using the Friedel–Crafts-type reaction. This makes use of an acid catalyst and an alkene. With ethene, for example, benzene forms ethylbenzene:

$$\bigcirc + H_2C = CH_2 \longrightarrow \bigcirc\text{---}CH_2CH_3$$

The formation of sulphonic acids

Benzenesulphonic acid is made by refluxing benzene with concentrated sulphuric acid:

$$\bigcirc + H_2SO_4 \longrightarrow \bigcirc\text{---}SO_2OH + H_2O$$

The sodium salts of alkylbenzenesulphonic acids are used as detergents.

SAQ 2.13

Draw structural formulae for the likely products formed by monosubstitution on methylbenzene of **a** ethene and **b** sulphuric acid.

Oxidation of substituted benzenes

Alkylbenzenes are oxidised to benzoic acid on prolonged reflux with acidified potassium manganate(VII). Benzoic acid is the aromatic product regardless of the length of the alkyl chain. The equation for the oxidation of methylbenzene is:

$$\bigcirc\text{---}CH_3 + 3[O] \longrightarrow \bigcirc\text{---}CO_2H + H_2O$$

On cooling the reaction mixture, benzoic acid separates out as a white crystalline solid (*figure 2.19*).

● *Figure 2.19* Benzoic acid crystallising.

SUMMARY

- Crude oil and natural gas are our main sources of hydro-carbons, which provide us with fuels and are the source of many other compounds of social and economic importance.

- Primary distillation of crude oil is followed by cracking, re-forming or isomerisation to obtain more useful alkanes and alkenes from high-molecular-mass hydrocarbons.

- All vehicles running on fossil fuels make a substantial contribution to the increase in the concentration of carbon dioxide in the atmosphere, and hence to the 'greenhouse effect'. Their emissions also include other, more immediately harmful, pollutants including carbon monoxide, nitrogen(II) oxide and hydrocarbons. Under certain weather conditions, reactions involving these pollutants and ultraviolet light produce photochemical smog. This contains a number of other, particularly irritating, gases such as ozone and peroxyacetyl nitrate (PAN).

- The geometry and structure of alkanes, alkenes and arenes (including the electron delocalisation model) may be described in terms of σ and π bonds. Hydrocarbons with σ bonds only are saturated hydrocarbons, those with both σ and π bonds are unsaturated hydrocarbons.

- Alkanes are non-polar molecules with strong bonds. They are thus relatively inert and their reactions have high activation energies. All alkanes are potential fuels as their reactions are highly exothermic.

- Alkanes react with free radicals such as chlorine or bromine atoms, which are produced by the photodissociation of chlorine or bromine molecules. These free radicals replace hydrogen atoms in the alkanes by an electrophilic substitution, forming chloro- or bromoalkanes.

- Alkenes are more reactive than alkanes because they contain a π bond. Under suitable conditions, addition reactions occur with hydrogen, water, hydrogen halides and halogens. Alkene molecules may also join to each other to produce polymers.

- Oxidation of an alkene under mild conditions breaks the π bond to form a diol. More vigorous oxidising conditions break the double bond, producing two organic products, which may be ketones or carboxylic acids.

- Alkenes exhibit *cis–trans* or geometric isomerism, because rotation about the double bond is prevented.

- Arenes have considerable energetic stability because of the delocalised π electrons. Arenes require much more vigorous reaction conditions to undergo addition reactions because of this extra stability.

- Arene chemistry is dominated by substitution reactions that enable arenes to retain the delocalised π electrons. Hydrogen atoms on the benzene ring may be replaced by a variety of other atoms or groups including halogen atoms, nitro ($-NO_2$) groups, alkyl groups or sulphonic acid ($-SO_2OH$) groups.

- Substitution on methylbenzene takes place at the 2, 4 and/or 6 positions.

- Oxidation of alkyl-substituted benzene always produces benzoic acid, whatever alkyl group is present.

- The variety of substitution reactions on benzene provides access to many useful compounds including medicines, dyes, explosives and polymers.

- Substitution on alkanes proceeds by a free-radical mechanism; substitution on arenes proceeds by an electrophilic mechanism. Electrophilic attack on an alkene results in addition reactions.

Questions

1 The following diagrams show the structures of four isomers of molecular formula C_4H_{10}.

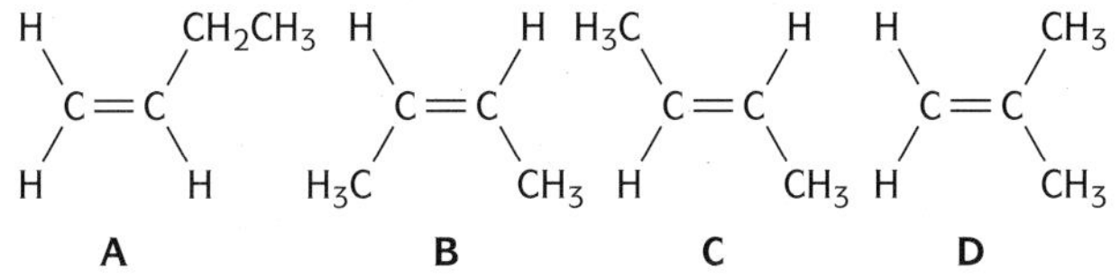

```
 H    CH₂CH₃  H      H  H₃C         H   H        CH₃
  \   /        \    /      \       /     \       /
   C=C          C=C         C=C          C=C
  /   \        /    \      /     \      /     \
 H     H     H₃C    CH₃   H      CH₃   H       CH₃

    A            B            C            D
```

a (i) To which class of compounds do the four isomers belong?

(ii) Which two diagrams show compounds that are *cis–trans* isomers?

b Compound **A** reacts with hydrogen bromide.

(i) Draw the displayed formula of the product and give its systematic name.

(ii) What type of reaction has taken place?

(iii) What type of mechanism is involved?

c Compound **B** produces one product on refluxing with an excess of concentrated, acidified potassium manganate(VII).

(i) What type of reaction has occurred?

(ii) Draw the structural formula for this product and label it with its systematic name.

2 a (i) Benzene can be nitrated using a mixture of concentrated nitric acid and concentrated sulphuric acid. Suggest how the nitration might be carried out. In your account, include reference to the apparatus used and the conditions required for the reaction to occur.

(ii) Describe the mechanism of the nitration, including reference to the generation of the nitrating species.

b State and explain the ways in which the substitution and addition reactions of benzene with chlorine

(i) are similar to and

(ii) differ from

those of cyclohexene with chlorine.

Chapter three

Halogen derivatives

By the end of this chapter you should be able to:

1 show awareness of the concern about the effect of chlorofluoroalkanes on the ozone layer;

2 recall the chemistry of halogenoalkanes as exemplified by: **a** the nucleophilic substitution reactions of bromoethane, including hydrolysis, the formation of primary amines by reaction with ammonia and the formation of nitriles, and **b** the elimination of hydrogen bromide from 2-bromopropane;

3 describe the mechanism of nucleophilic hydrolysis in halogenoalkanes;

4 interpret the different reactivities of halogenoalkanes and chlorobenzene with particular reference to hydrolysis and to the relative strengths of the C–X bonds;

5 explain the uses of fluoroalkanes and fluorohalogenoalkanes in terms of their relative chemical inertness, with reference to chlorofluoroalkanes, anaesthetics, flame retardants and plastics.

This chapter deals with the properties and reactions of the simple halogenoalkanes. These have the general formula $C_nH_{2n+1}X$, where X is a halogen atom: one of F, Cl, Br or I. They are named by prefixing the name of the alkane with fluoro, chloro, bromo or iodo and a number to indicate the position of the halogen on the hydrocarbon chain. For example, $CH_3CH_2CHClCH_3$ is 2-chlorobutane.

SAQ 3.1

Name the following compounds: $CH_3CH_2CH_2I$, $CH_3CHBrCH_3$ and $CBrF_2CBrF_2$.

Trouble in the ozone layer

You have probably heard about more complex halogenoalkanes such as CFCs. Chlorofluorocarbons (CFCs) are regularly blamed for causing damage to our environment. Although they absorb much more infrared radiation per molecule than carbon dioxide, their contribution to the 'greenhouse effect' is very low due to their very low abundance in the atmosphere (carbon dioxide is the main cause of the 'greenhouse effect'). More importantly, CFCs are responsible for a thinning of the protective ozone layer *(figure 3.1)* in the stratosphere. (Ozone absorbs significant quantities of harmful ultraviolet radiation and thus protects us from skin cancer.) CFCs are still used in air conditioners and were formerly used as refrigerants and aerosol propellants. They were chosen for these purposes as they are gases that liquefy easily when compressed. They are also very unreactive, non-flammable and non-toxic. (Before CFCs were used as refrigerants, highly toxic compounds such as ammonia or sulphur dioxide were used in domestic refrigerators. Leakage of ammonia or sulphur dioxide caused a number of deaths in the 1920s. As a result, some parts of the USA took the drastic measure of banning these early domestic refrigerators.)

The high stability of CFCs has been part of the cause of the problems in the ozone layer. This has

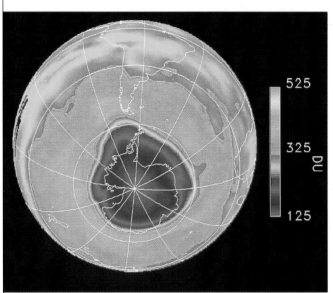

● **Figure 3.1** Representation of satellite measurements of the ozone 'hole' over Antarctica. Ozone concentration is measured in Dobson units (DU). The depletion of ozone reaches a maximum in October, the Antarctic spring, and is probably due mainly to the effects of chlorofluorocarbons (CFCs).

enabled concentrations of CFCs to build up in the atmosphere. When they reach the stratosphere, CFCs absorb ultraviolet radiation, which causes **photodissociation** of carbon–chlorine bonds. For example:

$$CF_2Cl_2(g) \xrightarrow{hf} CF_2Cl\cdot(g) + Cl\cdot(g)$$

Very reactive chlorine free radicals, $Cl\cdot(g)$, are formed. These radicals initiate a chain reaction with ozone:

$$Cl\cdot(g) + O_3(g) \longrightarrow ClO\cdot(g) + O_2(g)$$
$$ClO\cdot(g) + O_3(g) \longrightarrow Cl\cdot(g) + 2O_2(g)$$

The overall reaction equation is:

$$2O_3(g) \longrightarrow 3O_2(g)$$

The chlorine radicals are regenerated, so they act like a catalyst, and a few chlorine radicals can cause the destruction of large numbers of ozone molecules.

In 1928, Thomas Midgeley (an American engineer) was asked to find a safer alternative to the early refrigerants sulphur dioxide and ammonia. He suggested the use of CF_2Cl_2 and demonstrated its lack of flammability and lack of toxicity by inhaling the gas and blowing out a candle! Nowadays, chemists are designing new 'ozone-friendly' molecules to replace the destructive CFCs. The compound 1,1,1,2-tetrafluoroethane, CF_3CH_2F, is now being manufactured as an appropriate alternative. The presence of the hydrogen atoms increases the reactivity of this compound relative to CFCs, so that it is broken down in the lower atmosphere much more rapidly. If it does reach the stratosphere, it does not produce the damaging chlorine free radicals.

The classification of halogenoalkanes

Halogenoalkanes are classified according to their structures (*figure 3.2*).

■ In a **primary halogenoalkane** such as 1-chlorobutane, the halogen atom is covalently bonded to a carbon atom which, in turn, has a covalent bond to just *one* other carbon atom.

■ In a **secondary halogenoalkane** such as 2-chlorobutane, the halogen atom is covalently bonded to a carbon atom which, in turn, has covalent bonds to *two* other carbon atoms.

■ In a **tertiary halogenoalkane** such as 2-chloro-2-methylpropane, the halogen atom is covalently bonded to a carbon atom which, in turn, has covalent bonds to *three* other carbon atoms.

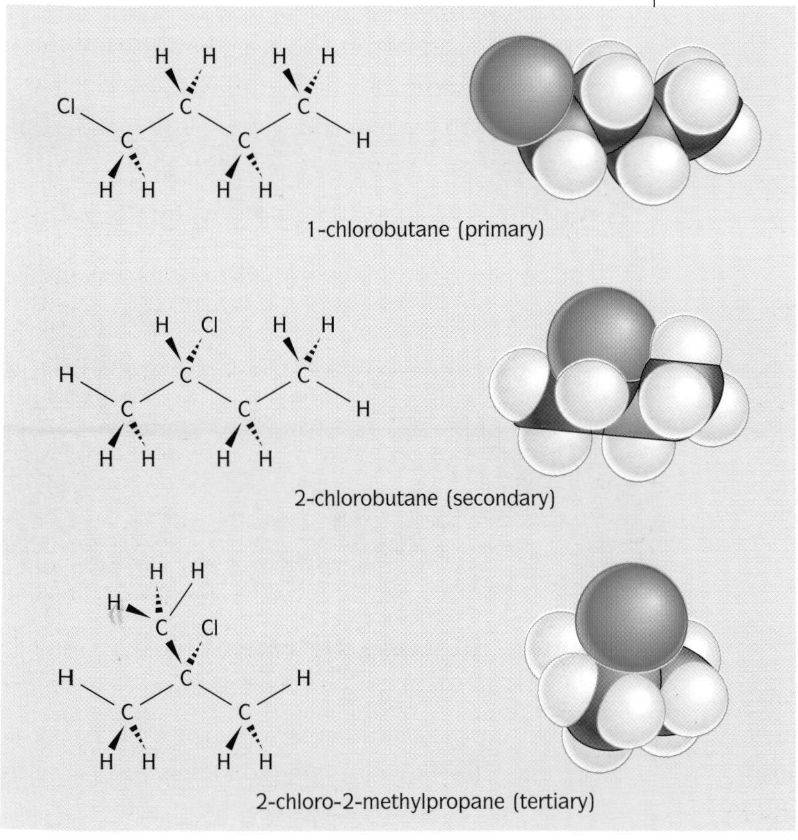

SAQ 3.2

What type of isomerism is shown by the compounds in *figure 3.2*?

Draw the structural formula of one further isomer of C_4H_9Cl. Is this a primary, a secondary or a tertiary chloroalkane?

1-chlorobutane (primary)

2-chlorobutane (secondary)

2-chloro-2-methylpropane (tertiary)

● **Figure 3.2** The classification of halogenoalkanes as primary, secondary or tertiary.

Other halogeno-compounds are shown in *figure 3.3*.

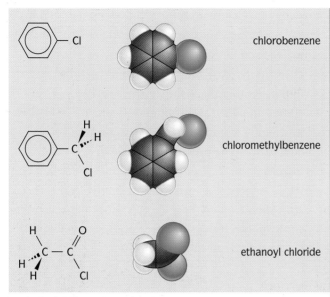

● *Figure 3.3* Some organic halogen compounds.

Physical properties

Typically, halogenoalkanes and halogenoarenes are volatile liquids that do not mix with water.

SAQ 3.3

a Explain why 1-chloropropane, C_3H_7Cl, is a liquid at room temperature (boiling point = 46.7 °C) whereas butane, C_4H_{10}, is a gas (boiling point = 0 °C).

b Why is it that halogen compounds such as 1-chloropropane do not mix with water?

Nucleophilic substitution

The predominant type of chemical reaction shown by halogenoalkanes involves substitution of the halogen by a variety of other groups. As the halogen atom is more electronegative than carbon, the carbon–halogen bond is polar:

In a substitution reaction, the halogen atom will leave as a halide ion. This means that the atom or group of atoms replacing the halogen atom must possess a lone-pair of electrons. This lone-pair is attracted to the slightly positive, δ+, carbon atom, and a new covalent bond forms. A chemical that can

donate a lone-pair of electrons, with the subsequent formation of a covalent bond, is called a **nucleophile**.

The mechanism for the nucleophilic substitution of bromine in bromomethane by a hydroxide ion is:

Nucleophilic attack is followed by loss of the bromine atom as a bromide ion. A new covalent bond between the nucleophile and carbon is formed. Overall a substitution reaction has occurred.

Some nucleophiles possess a net negative charge but this is not necessary for nucleophilic behaviour. Nucleophiles which will substitute for the halogen atom in halogenoalkanes include water, the hydroxide ion, ammonia and the cyanide ion. The conditions and equations for these reactions follow.

Hydrolysis

As the halogenoalkanes do not mix with water, they are mixed with ethanol before being treated with dilute aqueous sodium hydroxide. Warming the mixture causes a nucleophilic substitution to occur. The same hydrolysis reaction will occur more slowly without alkali, if the halogenoalkane is mixed with ethanol and water. The equation for the hydrolysis of bromoethane with alkali is:

$$CH_3CH_2Br + OH^- \longrightarrow CH_3CH_2OH + Br^-$$

The equation for the hydrolysis of bromoethane with water is:

$$CH_3CH_2Br + H_2O \longrightarrow CH_3CH_2OH + HBr$$

SAQ 3.4

Write a balanced equation for the alkaline hydrolysis of 2-bromo-2-methylpropane, using structural formulae for the organic compounds. Name the organic product.

Factors affecting the rate of hydrolysis

■ *Effect of halogen*

Hydrolysis gets easier as you change the halogen from chlorine to bromine to iodine. At first sight this may seem strange, since the polarity of the carbon–halogen bond decreases from chlorine to iodine. You might expect that a less positively charged carbon atom would react less readily with the nucleophilic hydroxide ion.

However, examination of the carbon–halogen bond energies *(table 3.1)* shows that the strength of the bond decreases significantly from C–Cl to C–I. This suggests that the ease of breaking the carbon–halogen bond is more important than the size of the positive charge on the carbon atom. A nucleophile may be attracted more strongly to the carbon atom but, unless it forms a stronger bond to carbon, it will not displace the halogen.

The carbon–fluorine bond does not undergo nucleophilic substitution because it is the strongest carbon–halogen bond. Despite its high polarity, no nucleophile will displace it. This accounts for the very high stability of the fluoroalkanes.

You can observe the relative rates of hydrolysis of halogenoalkanes by adding aqueous silver nitrate to the reaction mixture and timing the first appearance of a silver halide precipitate *(figure 3.4)*. This will form as soon as sufficient halogenoalkane has been hydrolysed. For example:

$$Ag^+(aq) + Cl^-(aq) \longrightarrow AgCl(s)$$

■ *Effect of hydrocarbon group*
Unlike the chloroalkanes, chlorobenzene will not hydrolyse with aqueous alcoholic alkali, even when refluxed for several hours. It can only be hydrolysed to phenol by heating with molten potassium hydroxide under pressure:

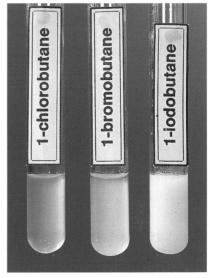

This greatly reduced reactivity may be explained in terms of electron delocalisation over the benzene ring. The delocalised π electrons tend to repel an attack by a nucleophile. The delocalised electron system on benzene also attracts electron charge away from the chlorine atom into the carbon–chlorine bond; the bond is strengthened. The increased strength causes a reduction in the length of the C–Cl bond from an average value of 0.177 nm in chloroalkanes to 0.170 nm in chlorobenzene.

Reaction with ammonia

If halogenoalkanes are mixed with alcoholic ammonia and heated under pressure, amines are formed. For example, bromoethane will form ethylamine:

$$CH_3CH_2Br + NH_3 \longrightarrow CH_3CH_2NH_2 + HBr$$

The ethylamine formed is a stronger nucleophile than ammonia. This is because of the positive inductive effect (page 17) of alkyl

Bond	Bond energy/kJ mol^{-1}
C–F	467
C–Cl	340
C–Br	280
C–I	240

● **Table 3.1** Bond energies of carbon–halogen bonds

● **Figure 3.4** The reaction of aqueous ethanolic silver nitrate with halogenoalkanes.

groups. Electron charge is pushed towards the nitrogen, making the nitrogen lone-pair even more available for nucleophilic attack and covalent bond formation, so reaction is possible. This is encouraged by an excess of bromoethane:

$$CH_3CH_2Br + CH_3CH_2NH_2 \\ \longrightarrow (CH_3CH_2)_2NH + HBr$$

The diethylamine produced is an example of a secondary amine. Ethylamine is a primary amine.

SAQ 3.5

Explain why ammonia behaves as a nucleophile in the formation of ethylamine, and give a mechanism for this reaction. What will happen to the hydrogen bromide formed?

Each additional alkyl group further enhances the nucleophilic strength of the amine formed and two further reaction steps are possible, given sufficient bromoethane. Triethylamine, a tertiary amine, is formed in the first of these:

$$CH_3CH_2Br + (CH_3CH_2)_2NH$$
$$\longrightarrow (CH_3CH_2)_3N + HBr$$

Amines, like ammonia, can form salts. A fourth bromoethane molecule produces a quaternary ammonium salt, tetraethylammonium bromide:

$$CH_3CH_2Br + (CH_3CH_2)_3N$$
$$\longrightarrow (CH_3CH_2)_4N^+Br^-$$

Reaction with cyanide ions

Refluxing halogenoalkanes with an aqueous alcoholic solution of sodium cyanide causes the halogen atom to be substituted by the cyanide ion. Organic compounds covalently bonded to cyanide are called **nitriles**. Notice that it is the cyanide carbon atom that bonds to the alkyl group, rather than the nitrogen atom. For example, bromoethane forms propanenitrile:

$$CH_3CH_2Br + CN^- \longrightarrow CH_3CH_2CN + Br^-$$

You should note that the additional carbon atom means the stem of the name changes from ethane to propane.

SAQ 3.6

a Draw a dot-and-cross diagram of the cyanide ion.

b Show how this can undergo a nucleophilic substitution reaction with bromoethane to form propanenitrile.

c What feature of the cyanide ion might lead to an alternative substitution product, CH_3CH_2NC (propaneisonitrile)? Suggest an explanation as to why propanenitrile is formed rather than the isonitrile.

Elimination reactions

Halogenoalkanes undergo nucleophilic substitution reactions with aqueous alcoholic sodium hydroxide to produce alcohols. However, if halogenoalkanes are refluxed with a purely alcoholic solution of sodium hydroxide, a different reaction occurs. For example, bromoethane will produce ethene:

$$CH_3CH_2Br + NaOH$$
$$\longrightarrow CH_2{=}CH_2 + NaBr + H_2O$$

This involves the base-catalysed elimination of a hydrogen halide, leaving an alkene. The hydrogen halide is neutralised by the alkali. Under these conditions, the rate of the elimination reaction is faster than the rate of the nucleophilic substitution reaction. At lower temperatures, the substitution reaction proceeds at a faster rate.

The uses of halogen compounds

As a functional group, the halogen atom provides chemists with useful routes to the synthesis of other compounds. This is a more important use of organic halogen compounds than their usefulness as products in themselves. For example, the synthesis of a medicine such as ibuprofen requires alkyl groups to be joined to benzene. This is achieved by Friedel–Crafts-type reactions (page 35) between halogenoalkanes and benzene. Ibuprofen is an anti-inflammatory medicine that brings relief to many people suffering from rheumatoid arthritis (which causes painful inflammation of the joints).

Halogenoalkanes which do have direct applications include the polymers poly(chloroethene) and poly(tetrafluoroethene) (*figure 3.5*); several CFCs,

● *Figure 3.5* Poly(tetrafluoroethene), PTFE, is used in the non-stick coating on saucepans and in waterproof clothing.

for example, dichlorodifluoromethane or trichlorofluoromethane, which are used as refrigerants, aerosol propellants or blowing agents (for producing foamed polymers); anaesthetics such as halothane, $CF_3CHClBr$; and firefighting compounds such as bromochlorodifluoromethane *(figure 3.6)*. The presence of a halogen atom confers flame-retarding qualities on the product. Bromochlorodifluoromethane (or BCF), CF_2BrCl, has been used in some fire extinguishers. The high temperatures in fires break this compound down, producing free radicals such as $Br\bullet(g)$. These react rapidly with other free radicals produced during combustion, quenching the flames.

● *Figure 3.6* Bromochlorodifluoromethane, BCF, is very effective at extinguishing fires. However, it is not now in general use because the breakdown products are poisonous.

SUMMARY

■ Halogenoalkanes have the general formula $C_nH_{2n+1}X$, where X is F, Cl, Br or I. They are named by prefixing the name of the alkane with fluoro, chloro, bromo or iodo and a number to indicate the position of the halogen on the hydrocarbon chain.

■ Chlorofluoroalkanes continue to be used extensively as they are inert, non-toxic, non-flammable compounds that have appropriate physical properties for use as propellants, refrigerants, blowing agents or cleaning solvents. Their unreactivity means that they stay in the atmosphere for a long time. They are broken down by ultraviolet radiation to release chlorine free radicals, which have reduced the concentration of ozone in the stratosphere.

■ Halogenoalkanes react with a wide range of nucleophiles. Nucleophiles possess a lone-pair of electrons, which is attracted to the positively charged carbon atom in a C–X bond. The halogen is substituted by the nucleophile, which forms a new covalent bond to the carbon atom attacked.

■ Bromoethane produces the following products on reaction with the following nucleophiles:
  ● ethanol on warming with water or aqueous alkali;
  ● ethylamine on heating under pressure with alcoholic ammonia;
  ● propanenitrile on refluxing with sodium cyanide.

■ The reactivities of different halogenoalkanes and chlorobenzene depend on the relative strengths of the C–X bonds. The C–F bond is very unreactive due to its high bond energy. The nature of the alkyl or aryl group affects both the polarity of the carbon atom and the strength of this bond (and hence its reactivity).

■ On heating 2-bromopropane with a strong base dissolved in ethanol, elimination of hydrogen bromide takes place and propene is formed.

■ Poly(tetrafluoroethene) (a fluoroalkane) is an important polymer valued for its inertness, high melting point and smooth, slippery nature. It is used for non-stick saucepans and electrical insulation. CF_3CH_2F is being introduced as a replacement for various CFCs in refrigerators and aerosol cans. Halothane, $CF_3CHClBr$, is used as an anaesthetic, and bromochlorodifluoromethane, CF_2ClBr, has been used in some fire extinguishers.

$\mathcal{Q}$uestions

1 The reactions outlined below refer to structural isomers of molecular formula C_4H_9Br.

  a Write a general equation for the hydrolysis of C_4H_9Br to give an alcohol.

  b **A, C** and **D** are structural isomers of molecular formula C_4H_9Br. Identify (by name or by structural formula) each of the compounds **A** to **F** below, using the information provided, giving an equation where required.

    (i) The alcohol obtained by hydrolysing **A** contains three methyl groups.

    (ii) The alcohol **B** is obtained by the hydrolysis of **C**, which has a chiral centre.

    (iii) Elimination of hydrogen bromide from **D** (by boiling it with concentrated ethanolic alkali) gives a single hydrocarbon **E**.
    D also reacts with sodium cyanide to give an unbranched compound **F**, C_5H_9N.

    Give the equations for the elimination of HBr from **D** and the reaction of **D** with sodium cyanide.

2 a (i) Outline the difference in the ease of hydrolysis of chlorobenzene compared with 1-chlorohexane. Give equations to explain any difference in the reactions taking place.

    (ii) Fluoroalkanes and chlorofluoroalkanes are families of important industrial chemicals. Using *table 3.1*, explain in terms of the strength and reactivity of the carbon–halogen bond why these compounds are relatively inert compared with the equivalent bromo- or iodo- compounds.

  b A sample of 1-bromopropane is divided into two portions. The first is warmed with aqueous potassium hydroxide, whilst the second is warmed with potassium hydroxide in ethanol. In each case a different product is formed. For each portion, identify the organic product, write an equation for the reaction, and explain the mechanism of the formation of the product.

  c Starting with bromoethane, outline how you would prepare a sample of propylamine.

  d Fluoroalkanes and chlorofluoroalkanes have many important uses which depend on their relative chemical inertness. Outline three such uses.

Chapter four

Hydroxy compounds

By the end of this chapter you should be able to:

1 describe and explain the production of ethanol by fermentation;

2 discuss the physiological effects of ethanol consumption;

3 recall the chemistry of alcohols, exemplified by the reactions of ethanol: **a** reaction with sodium, **b** esterification, **c** substitution to give halogenoalkanes, **d** oxidation to carbonyl compounds and carboxylic acids, **e** combustion, **f** dehydration to alkenes and **g** acylation;

4 describe the classification of hydroxy compounds into primary, secondary and tertiary alcohols;

5 suggest characteristic distinguishing reactions, for example mild oxidation;

6 describe the reactions of $CH_3CH(OH)-$ compounds which give tri-iodomethane with alkaline aqueous iodine;

7 discuss the uses of alcohols as fuels or solvents;

8 explain the relative acidities of water, phenol and ethanol;

9 recall the chemistry of phenol, as exemplified by the reactions: **a** with bases, **b** with sodium, **c** to form complex ions, **d** esterification and **e** halogenation of, and nitration of, the aromatic ring.

The homologous series of aliphatic alcohols has the general formula $C_nH_{2n+1}OH$. They are named by replacing the final '-e' in the name of the alkane with '-ol'. The position of the alcohol group is indicated by a number. For example, $CH_3CH_2CH(OH)CH_3$ is butan-2-ol. Aromatic alcohols are called phenols.

Fermentation and distillation

Ethanol has been known to humans in the form of alcoholic drinks for many thousands of years. If ripe fruit is harvested and left, fermentation of the sugar in the fruit will soon commence, producing ethanol and other compounds. Fermentation involves yeasts, which occur naturally on the skins of many ripening fruits such as grapes. It is quite probable that early humans, as hunters and gatherers, consumed alcohol by eating partially fermented fruit. It would have been quite a short step forward to allowing fruit (or partially germinated grain) to ferment in a container to form an alcoholic liquor. Such liquors would have a wide range of compounds present and would probably have given many of those people drinking them very sore heads!

Fermentation has become increasingly sophisticated *(figure 4.1)*. The process is an exothermic reaction which provides yeast with energy for its metabolism. Glucose (a sugar) is converted to ethanol and carbon dioxide by enzymes in the yeast:

$$C_6H_{12}O_6(aq) \longrightarrow 2C_2H_5OH(aq) + 2CO_2(g)$$

The reaction does not require oxygen (it is an **anaerobic** process), so fermentation is carried out with air excluded to prevent the oxidation of the ethanol to undesirable compounds such as aldehydes, which affect the flavour of the product and may cause headaches.

● **Figure 4.1** Stainless steel fermentation vessels at a modern winery.

In the 1980s and 1990s, there have been some major improvements in wine-making. One key improvement has been that the fermentation can be carried out at a lower temperature under nitrogen. These conditions can help to preserve the flavour of the fruit and have led to the production of many good quality wines at reasonable prices.

Fermentation stops when the ethanol concentration reaches about 15% by volume. This is because ethanol kills the yeast at this concentration. The higher concentration of alcohol found in spirits is produced by distillation of the fermented liquor.

The use and abuse of alcoholic drinks

Alcoholic drinks provide us with valuable nutrients, such as minerals and vitamins, as well as a source of energy. It has been estimated that almost 25% of dietary intake of energy (for both children and adults!) in seventeenth century Britain came from alcoholic drinks.

The ethanol in these drinks also affects our behaviour, and when drunk in excess may cause liver damage or even death. Whilst death may result from long-term alcohol abuse, it may also be caused from excessive short-term consumption, for example half a bottle of spirits drunk all at once. One reason people consume alcoholic drinks is because it makes them feel more relaxed and able to cope with stress. They generally feel more cheerful, less anxious and less tense. These effects are produced by the ethanol depressing the activity of the central nervous system.

Even small quantities of alcohol affect our ability to concentrate when driving motor vehicles or operating machinery. It has been shown that the intake of only one unit of alcohol may be sufficient to affect us. A unit of alcohol is a rough measure of the quantity of alcohol consumed. It is approximately:

- half a pint of beer;
- a glass of wine;
- a single measure of spirits.

The number of units required to raise the blood alcohol concentration (BAC) over the legal limit depends on a number of factors such as sex, body weight, age and how quickly it is consumed. As the driving ability of people is affected well before this limit is achieved it is clearly very unwise to consume anything containing ethanol before driving. The BAC can remain above the legal limit until the morning after drinking or even longer.

Miscibility with water

Miscibility is a measure of how easily a liquid mixes; it is the equivalent of solubility for solids. The miscibility of alcohols may be understood in terms of their ability to form hydrogen bonds to water. Methanol and ethanol are freely miscible in water in all proportions. When water and ethanol mix, some of the hydrogen bonds between the molecules in the separate liquids are broken. These are replaced by hydrogen bonds between water and ethanol. There is no significant gain or loss in energy. *Figure 4.2* shows a molecular model of hydrogen bonds between water and ethanol.

The miscibility of alcohols in water decreases with increasing length of the hydrocarbon chain. Although the hydroxyl group can still form hydrogen bonds to water, the long hydrocarbon chain disrupts hydrogen bonding between other water molecules. The hydrocarbon chains do not form strong intermolecular bonds with water molecules, because the hydrocarbon chains are essentially non-polar and only exert weak van der Waals' forces.

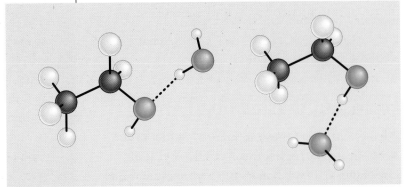

● **Figure 4.2** Hydrogen bonding between ethanol and water (the hydrogen bonds are represented by dotted lines). The bonds form between an oxygen lone-pair and a hydrogen atom.

Bond	Bond energy/kJ mol^{-1}
C–C	350
C–H	410
C–O	360
O–H	460

● *Table 4.1* Bonds and bond energies in ethanol

The reactions of alcohols

Alcohol reactions may be divided into groups, according to which bonds are broken. The bonds present in a typical alcohol such as ethanol are shown in *table 4.1*, together with their average bond energies.

SAQ 4.1

When a bond is broken, is the energy absorbed or released? Place the bonds in *table 4.1* in order of increasing strength.

Although the O–H bond is the strongest, it is also the most polar. The atoms involved in polar bonds are more susceptible to attack by polar reagents, so the O–H bond is not necessarily the most difficult bond to break in ethanol.

SAQ 4.2

a Apart from the O–H bond, which other bond in an alcohol is very polar?

b Why are this bond and the O–H bond so polar?

c Polar reagents include electrophiles and nucleophiles. Explain what is meant by each of these terms.

We shall now look at the reactions of alcohols in order, according to which bonds are broken.

Reactions in which the O–H bond is broken

Reaction with sodium

Metallic sodium reacts more gently with ethanol than with water, producing a steady stream of hydrogen. As ethanol is less dense than sodium, the metal sinks in ethanol, rather than floating as it does on water. The resulting solution turns phenolphthalein indicator pink (*figure 4.3*) and

● *Figure 4.3* Sodium reacting with ethanol. Phenolphthalein indicator has also been added. The pink colour shows that the alkaline ethoxide ion, $C_2H_5O^-$, has been formed.

produces a white solid on evaporation. The white solid is the ionic organic compound called sodium ethoxide, $CH_3CH_2O^-Na^+$. The equation for the reaction is:

$$2CH_3CH_2OH(l) + 2Na(s) \longrightarrow$$
$$2CH_3CH_2O^-Na^+(alcoholic) + H_2(g)$$

The $CH_3CH_2O^-$ ion is an ethoxide ion. In general, aliphatic alcohols produce alkoxide ions with sodium. This reaction may be compared to the reaction of sodium with water, in which one of the O–H bonds in a water molecule is broken, leaving a hydroxide ion:

$$2H_2O(l) + 2Na(s) \longrightarrow 2Na^+OH^-(aq) + H_2(g)$$

As sodium reacts more gently with ethanol than with water, industrial methylated spirit is used to safely destroy small quantities of sodium. You will find that industrial methylated spirit is used in school and college laboratories rather than pure ethanol. Pure ethanol is much more expensive and is subject to strict Customs and Excise control. Industrial methylated spirit contains ethanol with some methanol. It is similar to the purple methylated spirit sold for domestic use but it is colourless. Both are highly toxic due to the methanol content (methanol intake leads to blindness and death).

The reactivity of other aliphatic alcohols with sodium decreases with increasing length of the hydrocarbon chain. All reactions between aliphatic alcohols and sodium produce hydrogen and an ionic product. The organic anions formed have the general name alkoxide ions.

The formation of esters

When ethanol is warmed with ethanoic acid in the presence of a strong acid catalyst, an ester, ethyl ethanoate, is formed. This product smells strongly of pears. Other esters of aliphatic alcohols and carboxylic acids also have characteristic fruity odours. Many of these esters are found naturally in fruits. The equation for the formation of ethyl ethanoate is:

$$CH_3CH_2OH + H_3C - \overset{\overset{\displaystyle O}{\|}}{C} - OH \rightleftharpoons H_3C - \overset{\overset{\displaystyle O}{\|}}{C} - OCH_2CH_3 + H_2O$$

Concentrated sulphuric acid is usually used as the acid catalyst and the mixture is refluxed (page 11). The impure ester is obtained from the reaction mixture by distillation. The reaction mixture contains an equilibrium mixture of reactants and products.

Esters may also be prepared by reaction of an alcohol with an acyl chloride (**acylation**). Acyl chlorides react very vigorously and exothermically with alcohols, releasing hydrogen chloride gas. No catalyst is required and the reaction mixture may require cooling to slow down the reaction. The equation for the reaction of ethanol with ethanoyl chloride is:

$$CH_3CH_2OH + H_3C - \overset{\overset{\displaystyle O}{\|}}{C} - Cl \rightleftharpoons H_3C - \overset{\overset{\displaystyle O}{\|}}{C} - OCH_2CH_3 + HCl$$

You will find more about esters in chapter 6.

Reactions in which the C–O bond is broken

Substitution to form halogenoalkanes

When ethanol is heated with concentrated sulphuric acid and solid sodium (or potassium) bromide, bromoethane is formed. This method provides a standard route to other halogenoalkanes from the corresponding alcohols. You should bear in mind that halogenoalkanes are important intermediates in the formation of many other compounds (page 42).

Concentrated sulphuric acid and sodium bromide react to produce hydrogen bromide and sodium hydrogen sulphate. In the absence of an alcohol, the hydrogen bromide would escape as a gas:

$$NaBr(s) + H_2SO_4(l) \longrightarrow NaHSO_4(s) + HBr(g)$$

The hydrogen bromide acts as a nucleophile, substituting a bromine atom for the hydroxyl, –OH, group on the alcohol:

$$C_2H_5OH(l) + HBr(g) \longrightarrow C_2H_5Br(l) + H_2O(l)$$

Note that this reaction is the reverse of the hydrolysis of a halogenoalkane (page 40). Bromoethane distils from the hot liquid. The product is usually collected under water. Excess hydrogen bromide dissolves in the water. *Figure 4.4* shows the apparatus used to produce a small sample of bromoethane in the laboratory.

SAQ 4.3

a Draw a dot-and-cross diagram of hydrogen bromide.

b Indicate the polarity of the hydrogen bromide on your diagram.

c Draw the displayed formula for ethanol and indicate the polarity of the carbon–oxygen bond.

d Using curly arrows, draw diagrams to show the replacement of the hydroxyl group by a bromine atom.

e Complete your reaction scheme by showing the formation of water.

● *Figure 4.4* Bromoethane forms when a mixture of ethanol, concentrated sulphuric acid and sodium bromide crystals is heated. The product distils from the reaction mixture and collects as oily droplets under water.

SAQ 4.4

Compare the conditions for the hydrolysis of bromoethane with those for the reverse reaction. Explain how the different conditions enable the reaction to be reversed.

There are alternative methods of substituting a halogen atom in place of the –OH group:

■ *Reaction with a phosphorus halide*
Addition of a little phosphorus(V) chloride to ethanol produces misty fumes of hydrogen chloride. The reaction is strongly exothermic. As hydrogen chloride is easily identified – it turns blue litmus pink and produces a dense white smoke of ammonium chloride with ammonia gas (*figure 4.5*) – the reaction provides a quick, simple test for the presence of an –OH group. The equation for the reaction is:

$$CH_3CH_2OH(l) + PCl_5(s)$$
$$\longrightarrow CH_3CH_2Cl(l) + POCl_3(l) + HCl(g)$$

Bromo- or iodoalkanes may be produced by reacting alcohols with red phosphorus and bromine or iodine. These reagents effectively behave as PBr_3 or PI_3:

$$3CH_3CH_2OH + PBr_3$$
$$\longrightarrow 3CH_3CH_2Br + H_3PO_3$$

● *Figure 4.5* Ethanol reacting with phosphorus (V) chloride. The hydrogen chloride produced is detected using a drop of aqueous ammonia on a glass rod, which produces white fumes.

■ *Reaction with thionyl chloride*
This provides a particularly convenient route to chloroalkanes as the co-products are all gases:

$$CH_3CH_2OH(l) + SOCl_2(l)$$
$$\longrightarrow CH_3CH_2Cl(l) + SO_2(g) + HCl(g)$$

Reactions that also involve breaking C–C or C–H bonds

Mild oxidation

Like halogenoalkanes (page 39), aliphatic alcohols may be classed as primary, secondary or tertiary.

■ In a **primary alcohol**, the –OH group is on a carbon atom which is bonded to only *one* other carbon atom. Ethanol is a primary alcohol.
■ In a **secondary alcohol**, the –OH group is on a carbon atom which is bonded to *two* other carbon atoms.
■ In a **tertiary alcohol**, the –OH group is on a carbon atom which is bonded to *three* other carbon atoms.

Examples of primary, secondary and tertiary alcohols are:

$H_3C-CH_2-CH_2-OH$ propan-1-ol primary alcohol

propan-2-ol secondary alcohol

2-methylpropan-2-ol tertiary alcohol

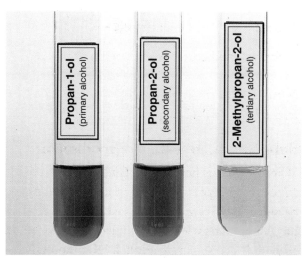

● *Figure 4.6* The colour changes that occur when primary, secondary and tertiary alcohols are treated with hot, acidified potassium dichromate(VI).

Primary and secondary aliphatic alcohols are oxidised on heating with acidified aqueous potassium dichromate(VI); tertiary alcohols remain unchanged with this reagent *(figure 4.6)*. As primary and secondary alcohols produce different, easily distinguished products, this reaction provides a useful means of identifying an unknown alcohol as primary, secondary or tertiary:

■ Primary alcohols produce aldehydes on gentle heating with acidified dichromate(VI). As aldehydes are more volatile than their corresponding alcohols, they are usually separated by distillation as they are formed. On stronger heating under reflux with an excess of acidified dichromate(VI), the aldehydes are oxidised to carboxylic acids.
■ Secondary alcohols produce ketones on gentle heating with acidified dichromate(VI).
■ Tertiary alcohols do not react with acidified dichromate(VI).

During the oxidation reactions, the orange colour of the dichromate(VI) ion, $Cr_2O_7^{2-}$(aq), changes to the green colour of the chromium(III) ion, Cr^{3+}(aq).

Ethanol produces the aldehyde ethanal on gentle heating with acidified dichromate(VI). You may prepare a sample of aqueous ethanal by distilling the aldehyde as it is formed when acidified dichromate(VI) is added dropwise to hot ethanol – simplified equations are frequently used for the oxidation of organic compounds, with the oxygen from the oxidising agent being shown as [O]:

$$CH_3CH_2OH + [O] \longrightarrow H_3C - \overset{\overset{\displaystyle O}{\|}}{C} - H + H_2O$$
ethanal

Ethanal has a smell reminiscent of rotting apples. Further oxidation, by refluxing ethanol with an excess of acidified dichromate(VI), produces ethanoic acid:

$$H_3C - \overset{\overset{\displaystyle O}{\|}}{C} - H + [O] \longrightarrow H_3C - \overset{\overset{\displaystyle O}{\|}}{C} - OH$$
ethanoic acid

You can separate aqueous ethanoic acid from the reaction mixture by distillation after it has been refluxing for 15 minutes. You can detect the ethanoic acid by its characteristic odour of vinegar and by its effect on litmus paper.

The secondary alcohol propan-2-ol, on gentle heating with acidified dichromate(VI), produces the ketone propanone. No other products can be obtained even with prolonged refluxing of an excess of the reactants.

$$H_3C - \overset{\overset{\displaystyle CH_3}{|}}{\underset{\underset{\displaystyle H}{|}}{C}} - OH + [O] \longrightarrow H_3C - \overset{\overset{\displaystyle O}{\|}}{C} - CH_3 + H_2O$$
propanone

Typically, ketones have pleasant odours resembling wood and fruit. Heptan-2-one is present in oil of cloves as well as in some fruits.

Complete oxidation: combustion

Ethanol is used as a fuel in the form of methylated spirit; it burns with a pale blue flame, but it is rather volatile and the flame is hard to see in sunlight, so accidents can occur when refilling stoves. Many campers favour it for cooking as it may be carried in lighter containers than those needed for gas. The equation for the complete combustion of ethanol is:

$$C_2H_5OH(l) + 3O_2(g) \longrightarrow 2CO_2(g) + 3H_2O(l);$$
$$\Delta H = -1367.3 \, kJ \, mol^{-1}$$

In some countries ethanol is blended with petrol to make a cheaper motor fuel. Methanol is used as a fuel for US Indycar racing.

Dehydration to alkenes

You can produce alkenes by eliminating hydrogen halide from halogenoalkanes or water from alcohols. For example, if ethanol vapour is passed over a hot, porous ceramic surface, both C–O and C–H bonds are broken producing ethene and water:

$$C_2H_5OH(g) \longrightarrow CH_2{=}CH_2(g) + H_2O(g)$$

The ceramic surface acts as a catalyst; the pores of the ceramic provide a large surface area. The high temperature, catalyst and large surface area all increase the rate of this reaction. The reaction is often referred to as **dehydration**, because a water molecule is removed. *Figure 4.7* shows how you can prepare a small sample of ethene by this method. (Note the similarity to the cracking of an alkane – see *Foundation Chemistry* (page 102).)

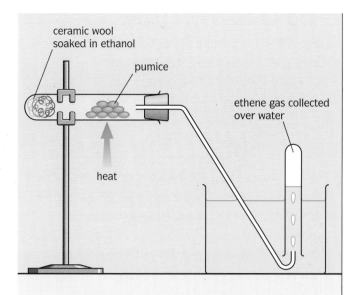

● *Figure 4.7*. The dehydration of ethanol.

An alternative method of eliminating water from an alcohol involves heating the alcohol with an excess of concentrated sulphuric acid at about 170°C. It is important to use an excess of acid, because an excess of ethanol leads to the formation of an ether (ethoxyethane) and water:

$$2C_2H_5OH(l) \longrightarrow C_2H_5OC_2H_5(l) + H_2O(l)$$

SAQ 4.5

a Draw the displayed formula for the organic product produced when propan-2-ol vapour is passed over a heated, porous ceramic surface.

b Write a balanced equation for this reaction.

The tri-iodomethane test

Some alcohols react with an alkaline solution of iodine. This involves breaking one C–C single bond and three C–H bonds to form tri-iodomethane, CHI_3. The reaction occurs only if $CH_3CH(OH)–$ is present in an alcohol (or $CH_3CO–$ in a ketone or in the aldehyde ethanal, CH_3CHO – see chapter 5). Tri-iodomethane forms as pale yellow crystals, and this provides a test for identifying the presence of these groups in these molecules. It is unusual to be able to identify a group such as $CH_3CH(OH)–$.

Ethanol works well in this test, which may be carried out as follows. Add aqueous dilute sodium

● *Figure 4.8* Tri-iodomethane crystals form when ethanol reacts with aqueous alkaline iodine.

hydroxide dropwise to aqueous iodine until the iodine is nearly colourless. Then add excess ethanol and warm the mixture for a few minutes in a water bath at about 50°C. Pale yellow crystals of tri-iodomethane are formed (*figure 4.8*). The reaction involves both oxidation and substitution:

$$CH_3CH_2OH(aq) + 4I_2(aq) + 6OH^-(aq) \longrightarrow$$
$$CHI_3(s) + HCOO^-(aq) + 5I^-(aq) + 5H_2O(l)$$

The uses of alcohols

■ Fuels

Alcohols have high enthalpies of combustion. The uses of ethanol and methanol as fuels have already been mentioned. Unleaded petrol contains about 5% of methanol and 15% of an ether known as MTBE (which is made from methanol). The rapid increase in the number of vehicles which can use unleaded fuel has made MTBE production grow faster than that of any other chemical.

■ Solvents

As alcohols contain the polar hydroxyl group and a non-polar hydrocarbon chain, they make particularly useful solvents. They will mix with many other non-polar compounds and with polar compounds. Methanol and ethanol will also dissolve some ionic compounds.

51

■ **Ethane-1,2-diol**

This compound is used as anti-freeze (for instance, to stop the water freezing in car radiators) and in polyester production. Polyester is made from two monomer units: benzene-1,4-dicarboxylic acid (terephthalic acid) and ethane-1,2-diol. The production of polyester involves ester formation between a hydroxyl group from ethane-1,2-diol and a carboxylic acid group from benzene-1,4-dicarboxylic acid. As each molecule possesses two of each group, a polymer chain forms. As each ester linkage results in the loss of a water molecule, this is an example of condensation polymerisation (page 87).

SAQ 4.6

a Draw the structure of ethane-1,2-diol.

b Explain why it mixes freely with water.

Phenols and their properties

Phenols, like alcohols, occur widely in nature. In phenols, the –OH group is joined to a benzene ring. Two very different examples are vanillin and estradiol.

■ Vanillin is found in the seed pods of the vanilla orchid. It is widely used as a flavouring in foods like chocolate or ice cream. The structure of vanillin is:

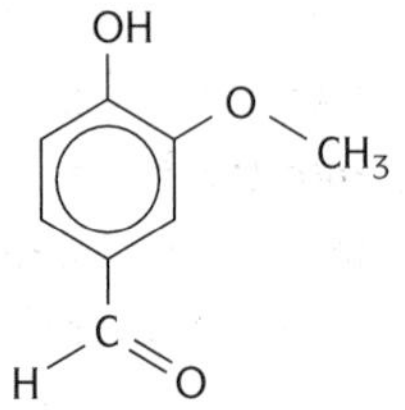

■ Estradiol is an important female sex hormone. It maintains female sexual characteristics and stimulates RNA synthesis (and hence promotes growth). Estradiol contains a secondary alcohol as well as a phenol. The structure of estradiol is:

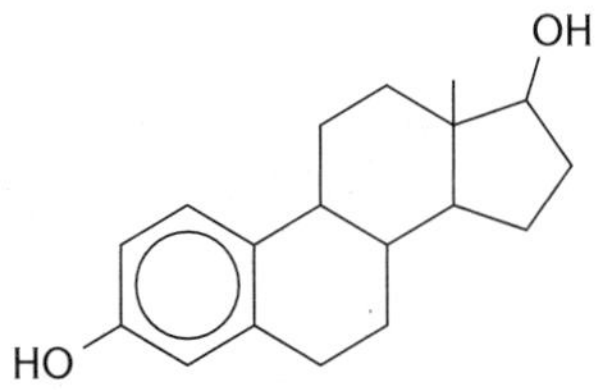

SAQ 4.7

a Copy the structures of vanillin and estradiol.

b Label the phenolic –OH group on each.

c Identify and label any other functional groups present.

Solubility in water

Phenol is sparingly soluble in water. The –OH group forms hydrogen bonds to water, whilst the benzene ring reduces the solubility because it forms only weak van der Waals' bonds to other molecules. Two liquid layers are formed if a sufficient amount of phenol crystals is added to water. The excess phenol absorbs water (again, by forming hydrogen bonds) and produces a lower liquid layer. This lower layer is a solution of water in phenol, the upper layer being a solution of phenol in water.

Reactions in which the O–H bond is broken

The reaction with bases

As phenol is a weak acid, it neutralises strong bases. For example, with sodium hydroxide the products are sodium phenoxide and water:

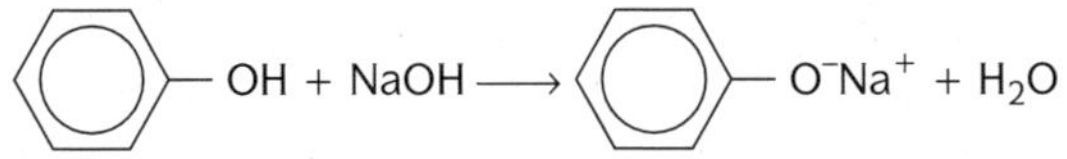

Sodium phenoxide is an ionic compound. Phenol dissolves completely in aqueous sodium hydroxide, but it is only sparingly soluble in water.

Addition of a strong acid to a solution of sodium phenoxide produces the reverse of the reaction with sodium hydroxide. Initially, a milky emulsion of phenol in water forms (*figure 4.9*). This is followed by phenol separating out as a dense, oily liquid layer. We can represent the equation as:

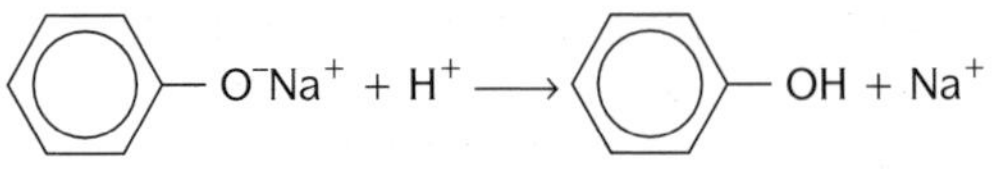

Reaction with sodium

Phenol reacts vigorously with sodium:

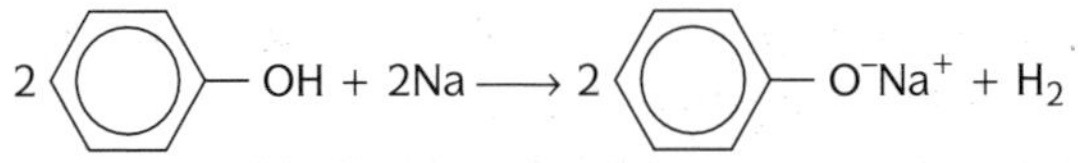

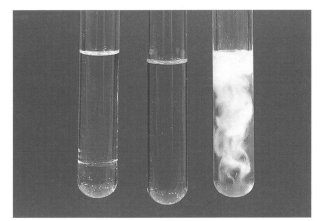

● **Figure 4.9** The left-hand tube shows phenol in water: the phenol does not mix, and settles out at the bottom of the tube. The central tube contains phenol dissolved in alkali. The right-hand tube shows the formation of a milky emulsion when the alkaline phenol is acidified.

Sodium phenoxide is formed and hydrogen is liberated. The greater reactivity (in comparison with ethanol) is again due to the weak acidity of phenol.

Complex ion formation

Phenols produce intense purple colours when treated with neutral iron(III) chloride (*figure 4.10*). These colours are due to the presence of complex

● **Figure 4.10** The reactions of phenol, a substituted phenol and ethanol with neutral iron(III) chloride.

ions, in which phenol forms dative covalent bonds to iron.

Esterification

Phenols do not react with carboxylic acids to form esters. This is because of the greater acidity of the phenols in comparison with aliphatic alcohols. Aromatic esters can be made by reacting phenols with acyl chlorides (page 69).

Reactions involving the benzene ring

Phenol undergoes electrophilic substitution reactions far more readily than benzene. The hydroxyl group, –OH, raises the electron charge density of the benzene π orbitals, considerably enhancing the reactivity of phenol towards electrophiles. The carbon–oxygen bond in phenol has about 16% double-bond character. This is caused by a partial delocalisation into the benzene ring of lone-pair electrons on the oxygen. The increased electron charge density is greatest at the 2, 4 and 6 positions on the ring.

Substitution with bromine

Aqueous phenol decolourises bromine water to form a white precipitate of 2,4,6-tribromophenol (*figure 4.11*):

The acidity of alcohols

Phenol ionises slightly in water. The O–H bond in phenol breaks to form a hydrogen ion and a negative phenoxide ion. This bond-breaking occurs more readily in a phenol molecule than in a water molecule, because the phenoxide ion is stabilised by a partial delocalisation over the benzene ring of the negative charge on the oxygen atom. Phenol is therefore more acidic than water.

$$\text{C}_6\text{H}_5\text{—OH} \rightleftharpoons \text{C}_6\text{H}_5\text{—O}^- + \text{H}^+$$

Ethanol ionises even less than water. The positive inductive effect in ethanol increases the electron charge density on the oxygen atom. This increases the ability of the ethoxide ion to attract hydrogen ions, so ethanol is less acidic than water.

The order of acid strength decreases as:

phenol (most acidic) > water > ethanol

All three are very weak acids in comparison to other weak acids that you may meet. Acids (or bases) which are fully ionised in solution are described as strong acids (or strong bases).

$$\text{OH} + 3\text{Br}_2 \longrightarrow \text{(2,4,6-tribromophenol)} + 3\text{HBr}$$

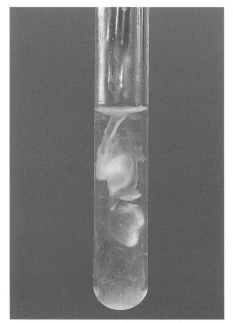

● **Figure 4.11** The reaction that occurs when bromine water is added to aqueous phenol.

Similar reactions occur with chlorine and iodine. Contrast these very mild conditions with the need to use pure bromine and pure benzene, together with an iron(III) bromide catalyst, to produce the mono-substituted bromobenzene.

SAQ 4.8

How does bromine in aqueous solution become sufficiently polar to achieve electrophilic substitution on phenol?

Nitration

If you heat phenol gently with dilute nitric acid, a mixture of 2- and 4-nitrophenols is formed:

$$\text{OH} + \text{HNO}_3 \longrightarrow \text{2-nitrophenol} + \text{H}_2\text{O}$$
or
$$\text{4-nitrophenol} + \text{H}_2\text{O}$$

Benzene requires the use of nitrating mixture (a mixture of concentrated nitric acid and concentrated sulphuric acid) and a temperature of 50–55 °C to produce nitrobenzene (page 33).

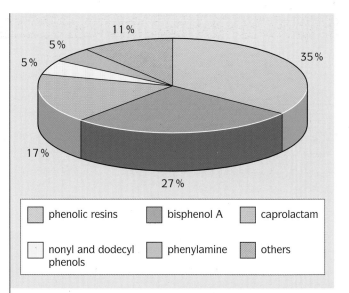

● **Figure 4.12** The major uses of phenol. Bisphenol A is produced by the reaction of phenol with propanone. It is an important chemical in the manufacture of polycarbonates and epoxy resins.

The use of nitrating mixture on phenol produces 2,4,6-trinitrophenol (picric acid). This is an unstable high explosive. It was used in shells and bullets by the Japanese during the Second World War. Many munitions workers lost their lives during the manufacture of these arms, because of the unpredictable nature of picric acid.

SAQ 4.9

Write a balanced equation for the formation of picric acid from phenol.

● **Figure 4.13** Compact discs, araldite and TCP are all manufactured using phenol as a raw material.

SUMMARY

- Ethanol has been used by humans for thousands of years in the form of alcoholic drinks, produced by the fermentation of sugar. Whilst alcoholic drinks are a valuable source of nutrients, excessive alcohol consumption may have serious consequences.

- Alcohols are soluble or partly miscible in water because hydrogen bonds can form between water molecules and the –OH group.

- Alcohol reactions may be grouped together by the bond(s) broken: the O–H bond, the C–O bond or the C–C and C–H bonds.

- The O–H bond is broken either by sodium to form an alkoxide and hydrogen or by carboxylic acids to form an ester and water.

- The C–O bond is broken by nucleophilic halides in, for example, hydrogen bromide or phosphorus(V) chloride.

- C–C and C–H bonds are broken by oxidation or elimination reactions and in the tri-iodomethane test.

- Oxidation of a primary alcohol occurs in two steps: an aldehyde is formed first and this is oxidised further to a carboxylic acid. Secondary alcohols are oxidised to ketones. Tertiary alcohols are not oxidised under mild conditions. Mild oxidation is usually achieved by heating the alcohol with acidified dichromate(VI).

- Elimination of water from an alcohol produces an alkene, the reaction is a dehydration. Dehydration may be carried out by passing ethanol vapour over a heated porous surface.

- Alcohols which contain the CH_3CHOH- group give pale yellow crystals of tri-iodomethane on warming gently with alkaline iodine.

- Complete oxidation of alcohols occurs on combustion to form carbon dioxide and water.

- Both methanol and ethanol are useful fuels. Alcohols are also used as solvents. Ethane-1,2-diol is used to make anti-freeze and polyesters.

- When the –OH group is joined directly to a benzene ring, the resulting alcohol is called a phenol.

- Phenols are acidic (relative to aliphatic alcohols) and form phenoxides on reaction with sodium hydroxide. The acidity of phenol is due to stabilisation of the negative charge in the phenoxide ion into the π electron system on the benzene ring.

- The reaction of sodium with phenol produces sodium phenoxide and hydrogen.

- The deep purple colour produced in the reaction between phenol and neutral iron(III) chloride is a useful test for a phenol.

- The –OH group enhances the reactivity of the benzene ring towards electrophiles. Bromine water is decolourised by phenol, producing a white precipitate of 2,4,6-tribromophenol. Nitric acid produces a mixture of 2- and 4-nitrophenols.

Questions

1 Pentyl ethanoate is used in the food industry as a flavouring agent in soft drinks. Its structure may be represented as:

$$H_3C - C \underset{OC_5H_{11}}{\overset{O}{\Vert}}$$

a Give the reagents and conditions to prepare a sample of this compound in the laboratory from pentan-1-ol.

b Draw the displayed formulae of a primary alcohol, a secondary alcohol and a tertiary alcohol that are isomeric with pentan-1-ol.

c What products, if any, would be formed if the three alcohols you have drawn in **b** were separately heated with an excess of acidified potassium dichromate(VI)? (Either names or structural formulae are acceptable answers.)

2 **a** (i) Describe, with the aid of diagrams, the origin of hydrogen bonding in organic compounds. Use ethanol as an example.

(ii) Describe how the concept of hydrogen bonding helps to explain why the solubility in water of ethanol differs from that of hydrocarbons of similar relative molecular mass.

b (i) Describe how would you attempt to convert ethanol to ethanoic acid in the laboratory. Give details of the reagents and the conditions under which the reaction should be carried out.

(ii) Draw a labelled diagram of the apparatus you would use to carry out the reaction.

c Describe and explain what you would observe when a few drops of ethanol are added to a small quantity of phosphorus(V) chloride. Give an equation for the reaction and name the organic product.

Chapter five

Carbonyl compounds

1 describe the formation of aldehydes and ketones from, and their reduction to, primary and secondary alcohols respectively;

2 describe the mechanism of the nucleophilic addition reactions of hydrogen cyanide with aldehydes and ketones;

3 describe the use of 2,4-dinitrophenylhydrazine to detect the presence of carbonyl compounds;

4 determine the nature (aldehyde or ketone) of an unknown carbonyl compound from the results of simple tests (the use of Fehling's and Tollens' reagents, and comparison of the ease of oxidation);

5 describe the reaction of CH_3CO- compounds with alkaline aqueous iodine to give tri-iodomethane.

You have encountered carbonyl compounds in chapter 4, in the form of aldehydes and ketones. Aldehydes are formed in the first stage of oxidation of primary alcohols whilst ketones are the only product formed on oxidation of secondary alcohols.

Both aldehydes and ketones contain the carbonyl group, C=O. In aldehydes, the carbon atom of this group is joined to at least one hydrogen atom. The aldehyde group is often written as –CHO. (This must not be confused with the hydroxyl functional group in alcohols, which is written as ⪢COH.) In ketones, the carbonyl group is joined to two other carbon atoms, so the simplest ketone, propanone, must contain three carbon atoms. *Table 5.1* shows the first few members of the homologous series of aldehydes

and ketones. Common names of these compounds are shown in brackets. Note that aldehydes are named by taking the alkane stem and replacing the '-e' with '-al'; with ketones the '-e' is replaced by '-one'.

Aliphatic aldehydes and ketones occur widely. The simple sugars, such as glucose and fructose, are present in aqueous solutions as equilibrium mixtures of chain and ring forms (*figure 5.1*). The chain form of glucose has an aldehyde group at

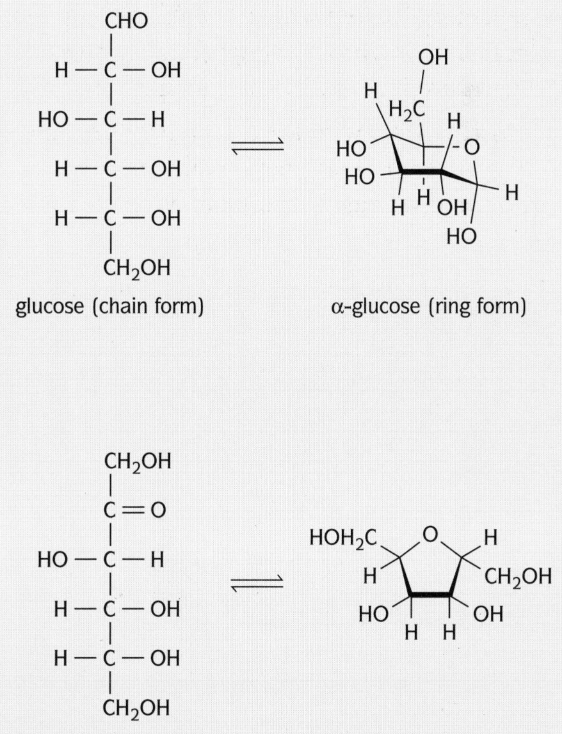

● **Figure 5.1** Chain and ring forms of sugars.

Aldehydes		Ketones	
Name	*Structural formula*	*Name*	*Structural formula*
methanal (formaldehyde)	HCHO		
ethanal (acetaldehyde)	CH_3CHO		
propanal	CH_3CH_2CHO	propanone (acetone)	$(CH_3)_2CO$
butanal	$CH_3CH_2CH_2CHO$	butanone	$CH_3COCH_2CH_3$

● **Table 5.1** The homologous series of aldehydes and ketones

● **Figure 5.2** The ketone, heptan-2-one, is responsible for the odour of blue cheese.

● **Figure 5.3** The very different flavours of spearmint, **b**, and caraway, **c**, are produced by the enantiomers of the ketone, carvone, **a**.

one end, whilst the chain form of fructose contains a ketone group. Aldehydes and ketones frequently contribute to the distinctive odours of foods and plants, though odour depends more on the overall shape of a molecule rather than on the functional groups present. Heptan-2-one is responsible for the odour of blue cheese (*figure 5.2*). Another example of a naturally occurring ketone is carvone. This is a chiral molecule and exists as two enantiomers (page 9) with very different odours. One enantiomer is responsible for the odour of spearmint, whilst the other is the principal odour in caraway seed (*figure 5.3*).

SAQ 5.1

Copy the structures for carvone and the chain forms of glucose and fructose. Label the aldehyde and ketone groups present. Mark the chiral carbon atom in carvone with an asterisk.

The simplest aromatic aldehydes are benzaldehyde, C_6H_5CHO, and phenylethanone, $C_6H_5COCH_3$:

benzaldehyde   phenylethanone

The aromatic carbonyl compounds have very distinctive, almond-like odours. Benzaldehyde is used to make almond essence, the flavouring used in Bakewell tarts and puddings. Benzaldehyde also contributes to the flavours of many fruits such as almonds, cherries, apricots, plums and peaches (*figure 5.4*). Such fruits contain amygdalin, $C_{20}H_{27}O_{11}N$. This molecule is hydrolysed by enzymes, forming benzaldehyde, glucose and hydrogen cyanide, HCN:

$$C_{20}H_{27}O_{11}N + 2H_2O \longrightarrow C_6H_5CHO + 2C_6H_{12}O_6 + HCN$$

● **Figure 5.4** Benzaldehyde contributes to the flavours of many fruits.

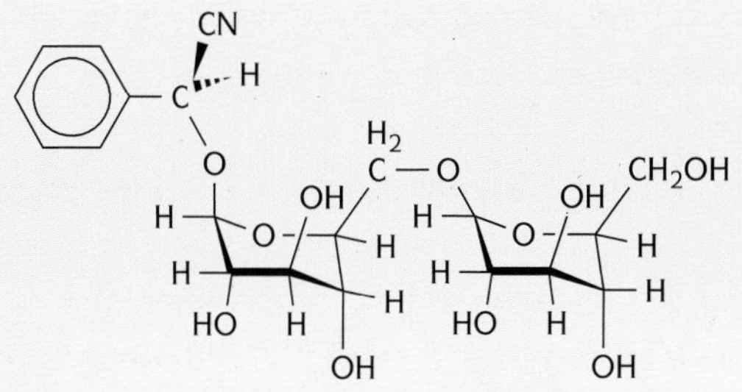

● **Figure 5.5** The structure of amygdalin.

Hydrogen cyanide is a toxic, colourless gas which also has an aroma of almonds. It contributes to the flavour of the fruits. Fortunately it is not a danger as it is only present at a very low concentration!

SAQ 5.2

Amygdalin is an example of a glycoside. Many different glycosides occur naturally in plants. They are built up from glucose and either an alcohol or phenol. The structure of amygdalin is shown in *figure 5.5*.

a Identify the parts of the amygdalin molecule which give rise to

   (i) hydrogen cyanide

   (ii) benzaldehyde

   (iii) glucose.

b Explain what is meant by the term *hydrolysis*.

Physical properties

The carbonyl group is significantly polar:

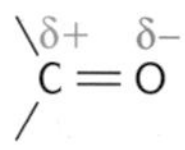

$$\overset{\delta+}{\underset{/}{\diagdown}}\!\!C = \overset{\delta-}{O}$$

The polarity is sufficient to enable the lower members of the homologous series of aldehydes and ketones to be completely miscible with water. Water will form hydrogen bonds to the carbonyl group:

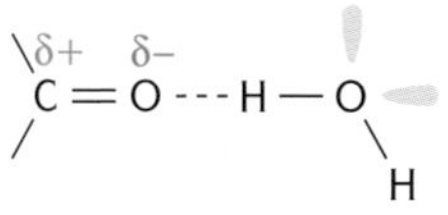

$$\overset{\delta+}{\underset{/}{\diagdown}}\!\!C = \overset{\delta-}{O} \cdots H - \overset{\displaystyle|}{\underset{H}{O}}$$

Explain the following in terms of intermolecular forces:

'Aldehydes and ketones containing more than four carbon atoms become increasingly immiscible with water.'

Redox reactions

Reduction

Aldehydes are obtained by mild oxidation of primary alcohols, and ketones are formed when secondary alcohols are oxidised (see chapter 4). Aldehydes or ketones may be reduced to their respective alcohols. Lithium tetrahydridoaluminate, $LiAlH_4$, is a suitable reducing agent. The aldehyde or ketone is warmed with the reducing agent using ethoxyethane as a solvent. (Alternatives to $LiAlH_4$ include sodium tetrahydridoborate, $NaBH_4$ or hydrogen under high pressure with a nickel catalyst.) It is usual to represent $LiAlH_4$ by [H] in the equation for the reduction. (Compare this to the use of [O] in the equations for the oxidation of alcohols with acidified dichromate(VI).) Here are two examples.

Ethanal is reduced to ethanol:
$$CH_3CHO + 2[H] \longrightarrow CH_3CH_2OH$$

Propanone is reduced to propan-2-ol:
$$CH_3COCH_3 + 2[H] \longrightarrow CH_3CH(OH)CH_3$$

The reactions may also be regarded as addition of hydrogen to the carbonyl double bond. Remember that hydrogen may also add to the carbon–carbon double bond in alkenes.

SAQ 5.4

Draw the structural formulae for the products obtained when the following are treated with hydrogen under pressure in the presence of a nickel catalyst:

a butanone;

b but-2-ene;

c butanal.

Oxidation

Under mild conditions, aldehydes are oxidised further to carboxylic acids. The aldehyde is usually refluxed with acidified potassium dichromate(VI). Ketones are not oxidised under these conditions. We have already studied the oxidation of primary alcohols to aldehydes and aldehydes to carboxylic acids in chapter 4 (pages 49–50), and you may find it helpful to revise that section now.

SAQ 5.5

Draw the displayed formula for the product formed when butanal is refluxed with acidified potassium dichromate(VI).

Addition of hydrogen cyanide

Both aldehydes and ketones will react with hydrogen cyanide. The product is a hydroxynitrile. For example, propanal will form 2-hydroxybutane-nitrile:

$$CH_3CH_2\text{\textbackslash}\,C=O + HCN \longrightarrow CH_3CH_2 - \overset{OH}{\underset{H}{C}} - C\equiv N$$

Notice that this reaction introduces an extra carbon atom into the molecule. Hence the stem name changes from propane to butane.

Unlike addition to alkenes, which involves an electrophilic mechanism (page 30), the polarity of the carbonyl compounds allows nucleophilic addition to occur. The reaction is catalysed by the presence of a base. Hydrogen cyanide is a very weak acid and the presence of a base increases the concentration of cyanide ions. The cyanide ion is a stronger nucleophile than hydrogen cyanide. The lone-pair of electrons on the carbon atom in the cyanide ion attacks the positively charged carbon atom of the carbonyl group:

$$\overset{\delta+}{C}=\overset{\delta-}{O} \longrightarrow -\overset{|}{\underset{CN:}{C}}-O:^{\ominus}$$
$$:CN:^{\ominus}$$

The intermediate ion rapidly reacts with a proton (either from an HCN molecule or from a water molecule in the solvent) to form the hydroxy-nitrile:

$$-\overset{|}{\underset{CN:}{C}}-O:^{\ominus} \quad H-CN: \longrightarrow -\overset{|}{\underset{CN:}{C}}-OH + :CN:^{\ominus}$$

The reaction has considerable synthetic importance due to the formation of a new carbon–carbon bond. The nitrile group is readily converted to a carboxylic acid by hydrolysis:

$$-\overset{|}{\underset{CN}{C}}-OH + 2H_2O \longrightarrow -\overset{|}{\underset{COOH}{C}}-OH + NH_3$$

Hydrolysis is achieved by refluxing with aqueous acid or aqueous alkali.

Alternatively, reduction of the nitrile group produces an amine:

$$-\overset{|}{\underset{CN}{C}}-OH + 4[H] \longrightarrow -\overset{|}{\underset{CH_2NH_2}{C}}-OH$$

Reduction is carried out either by using sodium in ethanol or by refluxing with lithium tetrahydrido-aluminate in ethoxyethane.

Characteristic tests

A test for the presence of the carbonyl group, C=O

When a solution of 2,4-dinitrophenylhydrazine is added to an aldehyde or a ketone, a deep yellow or orange precipitate is formed (*figure 5.6*). The test is

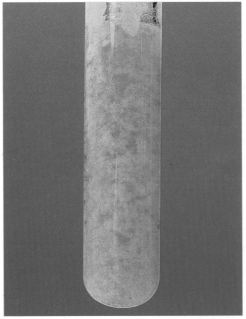

● **Figure 5.6** Propanone reacts with 2,4-dinitrophenyl-hydrazine to form a 2,4-dinitrophenylhydrazone.

quite specific for an aldehyde or ketone carbonyl bond. No precipitate is produced with carboxylic acids or with esters, although each of these classes of compounds contain carbonyl groups. The reaction involves an addition across the double bond followed by elimination of a water molecule. The yellow precipitate is a 2,4-dinitrophenylhydra*zone*. The equation for the reaction of ethanal with 2,4-dinitrophenylhydra*zine* is:

atoms lost in condensation reaction to form water

2,4-dinitrophenylhydrazine   2,4-dinitrophenylhydrazone

As water is eliminated in the formation of the carbon–nitrogen double bond in the hydrazone, the reaction is a condensation reaction. In general, a **condensation reaction** is one in which two molecules join together to form a larger molecule, with elimination of a small molecule (which is often water, but may be methanol, hydrogen chloride, ammonia, etc.).

We use 2,4-dinitrophenylhydrazine rather than phenylhydrazine because it gives better precipitates. These precipitates are easily recrystallised. Recrystallisation, followed by the determination of the melting point of the 2,4-dinitrophenylhydrazone product and determination of the boiling point of the aldehyde or ketone, can help to identify an unknown carbonyl compound.

Distinguishing between aldehydes and ketones

Aldehydes produce carboxylic acids when treated with mild oxidising agents. Ketones are not oxidised by these reagents. Suitable mild oxidising agents, together with the observations seen when they are used to oxidise an aldehyde, are shown in *table 5.2*. The observations are illustrated in *figure 5.7*.

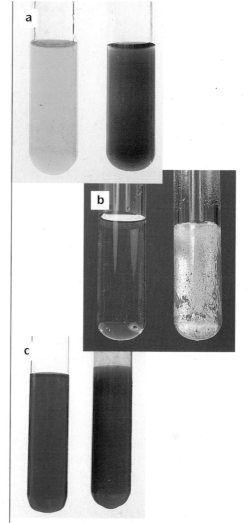

● **Figure 5.7** 'Before' and 'after' situations for the oxidation of ethanal by **a** acidified potassium dichromate(VI), **b** Tollens' reagent and **c** Fehling's solution.

Oxidising agent	Conditions	Observation on oxidation of an aldehyde	Explanation of observation
acidified potassium dichromate(VI)	boil gently (reflux)	the orange solution turns green	the orange dichromate(VI) ion, $Cr_2O_7^{2-}$, is reduced to green chromium(III) ion, Cr^{3+}
Tollens' reagent (an aqueous solution of silver nitrate in excess ammonia)	warm	a silver mirror forms on the sides of the test tube from the colourless solution	the colourless diammine silver(I) complex ion, $[Ag(NH_3)_2]^+$, is reduced to silver metal
Fehling's reagent (an alkaline solution of a complex copper ion)	boil gently	a brick-red precipitate forms from the deep blue solution	the blue copper complex ion is reduced to brick-red copper(I) oxide

● **Table 5.2** The effects of oxidising agents on aldehydes

The tri-iodomethane test

This is a very unusual test in that it identifies more than just a functional group. It is specific to compounds of the form CH₃COR (or, as it is carried out under mildly oxidising conditions, to CH₃CHOHR). When a compound having either of these groups is warmed gently (for example, in a water bath at about 40°C) with alkaline aqueous iodine, a pale yellow, crystalline solid forms (*figure 4.8*, page 51). The pale yellow product is tri-iodomethane, CHI₃. Its formation initially involves substitution of the three hydrogen atoms in the methyl group by iodine. For example, with ethanal:

$$CH_3CHO + 3I_2 \longrightarrow CI_3CHO + 3HI$$

This is followed by cleavage of the carbon–carbon bond by an alkali to form tri-iodomethane and a methanoate ion:

$$CI_3CHO + OH^- \longrightarrow CHI_3 + HCOO^-$$

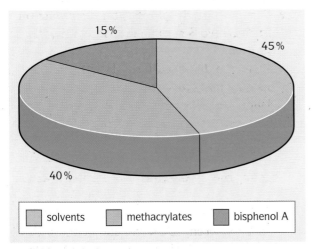

● **Figure 5.8** The major uses of propanone.

● **Figure 5.9** Methacrylate polymerises to a bright, transparent product that is used extensively in vehicle light clusters.

SAQ 5.6

a From the following compounds, identify those that will give a pale yellow precipitate when warmed with alkaline aqueous iodine:

   (i) CH₃COCH₃

   (ii) CH₃CH₂CHO

   (iii) CH₃CH(OH)CH₃

   (iv) CH₃CH₂OH

   (v) CH₃CH₂COCH₂CH₃

b For the compounds which give a precipitate, write the structural formulae of the organic products.

SUMMARY

■ Aldehydes and ketones contain the carbonyl group, C=O. In aldehydes the carbonyl group is joined to just one other carbon atom; in ketones the carbonyl group is joined to two other carbon atoms.

■ The systematic names of aldehydes are derived from the name of the alkane with the '-e' repaced by '-al'. Similarly ketones are named with the '-e' replaced by '-one'.

■ As the carbonyl group is very polar, aldehydes and ketones are water-soluble.

■ Reduction of an aldehyde produces a primary alcohol; reduction of a ketone produces a secondary alcohol.

■ Aldehydes are readily oxidised under mild conditions to carboxylic acids. Ketones are not oxidised under mild conditions.

■ The polar nature of the carbonyl group in aldehydes and ketones enables them to undergo nucleophilic addition of hydrogen cyanide to form hydroxynitriles.

■ The mechanism of nucleophilic addition involves attack on the carbon atom of a cyanide ion by a lone-pair of electrons. A covalent bond forms to the positively charged carbon atom of the C=O. The π bond breaks and produces a negative charge on the oxygen of the C=O, which removes a hydrogen ion from a hydrogen cyanide molecule, forming the hydroxynitrile and another cyanide ion. The reaction is catalysed by sodium cyanide.

■ The reagent 2,4-dinitrophenylhydrazine produces a yellow precipitate with aldehydes and ketones. A condensation reaction is involved (water is eliminated).

■ As aldehydes are readily oxidised, they may be distinguished from ketones on warming with suitable oxidising reagents: acidified potassium dichromate(VI) turns from orange to green; Tollens' reagent produces a silver mirror; and Fehling's solution forms a brick-red precipitate.

■ Aldehydes and ketones containing the $CH_3CO–$ group produce pale yellow crystals of tri-iodomethane on warming with an alkaline solution of iodine.

■ Propanone is an important solvent.

Questions

1 The following reactions were observed for compound **A** of formula C_3H_6O.
 I The compound did not react with alkaline aqueous copper(II) ions, even when heated.
 II On adding 2,4-dinitrophenylhydrazine, a yellow precipitate formed.
 III Reaction with hydrogen in the presence of a catalyst produced a colourless liquid **B**. Liquid **B** reacted with sodium to give hydrogen.
 a Draw the displayed formulae of two compounds of formula C_3H_6O.
 b What does the result of reaction **I** show?
 c The formation of the yellow precipitate in reaction **II** is a positive test for a particular organic group. Identify this group.
 d Using the formula of the compound and the results of reactions **I** and **II**, identify **A**.
 e Write balanced equations for the reduction of **A** to give **B** and the reaction of **B** with sodium.
 f Draw the displayed formula of **B**, and give its systematic name.
 g Under suitable conditions, **A** will react with hydrogen cyanide to form a compound of formula C_4H_7ON. State the type and mechanism of this reaction, giving the conditions for reaction to occur.

2 a Describe the similarities of, and the differences between, aldehydes and ketones. Use propanal and propanone as your examples. Give equations and details of reactants and products, where appropriate.
 b Describe the mechanism of nucleophilic addition to a carbonyl group, with the aid of an appropriate example.

Chapter six

Carboxylic acids and derivatives

By the end of this chapter you should be able to:

1 describe the formation of carboxylic acids from alde-hydes, nitriles and alcohols (including the production of vinegar);

2 show awareness of alternative sources of carboxylic acids;

3 describe the reactions of carboxylic acids in the forma-tion of salts, esters and acyl chlorides;

4 explain the acidity both of carboxylic acids and of chlorine-substituted ethanoic acids in terms of their structures;

5 describe the hydrolysis of acyl chlorides;

6 describe the reactions of acyl chlorides with alcohols, phenols and primary amines;

7 explain the relative ease of hydrolysis of acyl chlorides, alkyl chlorides and aryl chlorides;

8 describe the formation of esters from carboxylic acids or acyl chlorides, using ethyl ethanoate and phenyl benzoate as examples;

9 describe the acid and base hydrolysis of esters;

10 interpret the molecular structures of fats as natural esters;

11 describe the uses of esters.

The carboxylic acid functional group is –COOH. This consists of a hydroxyl group joined to a carbonyl group. Simple carboxylic acids are present in many foods. The sharp acidic taste of vinegar is caused by the ethanoic acid (acetic acid) present. Ethanoic acid has the formula CH_3COOH. The simplest aromatic carboxylic acid, benzoic acid, is used as a flavouring and a preservative in sparkling drinks such as lemonade. The acidity of lemons is caused by citric acid (*figure 6.1*). The structures of benzoic acid and citric acid are:

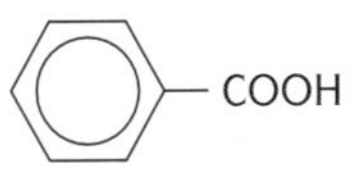

benzoic acid

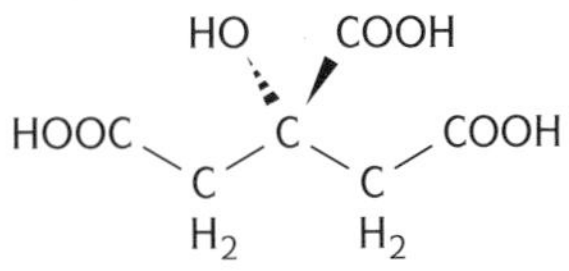

citric acid

Esters are derivatives of carboxylic acids and are present in many foods. In esters, the hydrogen in the carboxylic acid group is replaced by an alkyl or an aryl group. Aliphatic esters have distinctive, fruity flavours. They are one of the principal flavouring components in most fruits (*figure 6.2*): ethyl 2-methylbutanoate is one component

● *Figure 6.1* Lemonade often contains benzoic acid as a preservative. Citric acid is present naturally in lemons.

● *Figure 6.2* Esters are principal flavour components in ripe fruits.

of the flavour of ripe apples; 3-methylbutyl ethanoate contributes to the flavour of ripe pears.

ethyl 2-methylbutanoate   3-methylbutyl ethanoate

Acyl chlorides are also important derivatives of carboxylic acids. In an acyl chloride, the hydroxyl group of the carboxylic acid is replaced by a chlorine atom. Acyl chlorides are highly reactive and are used in organic synthesis to introduce the acyl group, RCO–, into other organic compounds. The structure of an acyl chloride is:

$$H_3C - C \overset{O}{\underset{Cl}{\diagdown}}$$

ethanoyl chloride

SAQ 6.1

Classify the following compounds as carboxylic acids, esters or acyl chlorides:

a $CH_3CH_2CH_2COOCH_3$

b $CH_2ClCOOH$

c $HCOCl$

Carboxylic acids

The structure of the carboxylic acid group is:

$$- C \overset{O}{\underset{OH}{\diagdown}}$$

Carboxylic acids are named by taking the name of the alkane and replacing the final '-e' with '-oic acid'. The first four members of the homologous series of aliphatic carboxylic acids are shown in *table 6.1*. Note that the carbon atom of the carboxylic acid is counted as a carbon atom from the parent alkane. The general formula for the aliphatic carboxylic acids is $C_nH_{2n+1}COOH$.

Structural formula	Systematic name	Common name
HCOOH	methanoic acid	formic acid
CH_3COOH	ethanoic acid	acetic acid
CH_3CH_2COOH	propanoic acid	propionic acid
$CH_3CH_2CH_2COOH$	butanoic acid	butyric acid

● **Table 6.1**   The first four members of the homologous series of carboxylic acids

Sources of carboxylic acids

Natural sources

Both petroleum fractions and natural oils provide sources of carboxylic acids. The naphtha crude oil fraction is an important starting material for making other chemicals; it is called a **feedstock**. Large quantities of ethanoic acid are made by the catalytic oxidation of naphtha.

Vegetable oils (*figure 6.3*) and animal fats are esters of carboxylic acids and the alcohol propane-1,2,3-triol (also known as glycerol). Hydrolysis of these oils or fats provides an important source of carboxylic acids with longer chains of carbon atoms. Some examples are shown in *table 6.2*.

In general, carboxylic acids that are obtained from oils or fats are called **fatty acids**. They usually contain an even number of carbon atoms and form unbranched chains. Fatty acids with one

● **Figure 6.3** Oleic acid can be obtained from olive oil, which contains an ester of oleic acid.

Common name	Systematic name	Skeletal formula	Principal source
lauric acid	dodecanoic acid	⋀⋀⋀⋀⋀COOH	coconut oil
myristic acid	tetradecanoic acid	⋀⋀⋀⋀⋀⋀COOH	nutmeg seed oil
stearic acid	octadecanoic acid	⋀⋀⋀⋀⋀⋀⋀COOH	animal fats
oleic acid	octadeca-*cis*-9-enoic acid	⋀⋀⋀⋁═⋀⋀⋀COOH	olive oil

● **Table 6.2** Some natural carboxylic acids

carbon–carbon double bond are said to be **mono-unsaturated**. They are polyunsaturated if they contain more than one carbon–carbon double bond (see page 27). Each double bond will give rise to geometric isomers.

Synthetic sources

In the laboratory, there are a variety of synthetic routes to carboxylic acids. These methods include the oxidation of primary alcohols or aldehydes (pages 49–50) and the hydrolysis of nitriles (page 60). The reduction of a carboxylic acid using lithium tetrahydridoaluminate produces a primary alcohol. For example, propanoic acid is reduced to propan-1-ol:

$$CH_3CH_2COOH + 4[H] \rightarrow CH_3CH_2CH_2OH + H_2O$$

SAQ 6.2

a Draw the skeletal formula of hexadecanoic acid (palmitic acid).

b Draw the skeletal formula and name the *trans* isomer of oleic acid.

c Name the following fatty acid:
⋀⋀⋁═⋁═⋀⋀⋀COOH

d Draw the displayed formula of and name the carboxylic acid formed on oxidation of 2-methylpropan-1-ol.

e Draw the displayed formula of and name the carboxylic acid formed on hydrolysis of propanenitrile.

f Name the product formed on treatment of 3-methylbutanoic acid with LiAlH$_4$. What type of reaction is involved? Write an equation for the reaction using structural formulae.

The reactions of carboxylic acids

You met the hydroxyl group in chapter 4, and the carbonyl group in chapter 5. In carboxylic acids these two groups combine to form the carboxylic acid functional group, –COOH. The combination of these two groups modifies the properties of each of them.

Behaviour as acids

The proximity of the polar carbonyl group enables the hydroxyl group to ionise partly in water. Hence carboxylic acids are weak acids – unlike alcohols, which do not ionise to any significant degree in water.

The ionisation of the carboxyl group is due to delocalisation of the negative charge over the carbon and oxygen atoms. This delocalisation increases the energetic stability of the anion, producing an equilibrium in aqueous solution:

$$R-C\overset{O}{\underset{O-H}{\diagdown}} (aq) \rightleftharpoons R-C\overset{O}{\underset{O}{\diagdown}}\!{}^{\ominus} (aq) + H^+(aq)$$

If the carboxylic acid –R group contains electronegative atoms such as chlorine, the electron-withdrawing ability of these groups further stabilises the anion. This increases the degree of ionisation (and hence the strength of the acid):

$$-\overset{|}{\underset{Cl}{C}} \leftarrow C\overset{O}{\underset{O}{\diagdown}}\!{}^{\ominus}$$

This is particularly apparent for the three substituted chloroethanoic acids shown in *table 6.3*. The quantity pK_a is a measure of the strength of an acid. The smaller the value of pK_a, the greater the degree of dissociation of the acid into ions. The pK_a value of a weak acid is high; the pK_a of a strong acid is low. Hence ethanoic acid is a weak acid; trichloroethanoic acid is a strong acid.

Acid	Structural formula	pK_a	Order of acid strength
ethanoic acid	CH_3COOH	4.8	
chloroethanoic acid	$CH_2ClCOOH$	2.9	increasing acid strength
dichloroethanoic acid	$CHCl_2COOH$	1.3	
trichloroethanoic acid	CCl_3COOH	0.7	

● **Table 6.3** The relative strengths of chlorine-substituted ethanoic acids

SAQ 6.3

Place the following carboxylic acids in order of increasing acid strength: CH_2FCOOH, $CH_2ClCOOH$, $CH_2BrCOOH$ and CH_2ICOOH.

Carboxylic acids form salts when reacted with metals (such as magnesium or zinc), alkalis, carbonates and basic metal oxides. In addition to producing a salt in the reaction with a carboxylic acid:

■ metals produce hydrogen;
■ alkalis and basic metal oxides produce water;
■ carbonates produce carbon dioxide and water.

For example, if you neutralise ethanoic acid with sodium hydroxide, sodium ethanoate and water are formed:

$$CH_3COOH(aq) + NaOH(aq)$$
$$\longrightarrow CH_3COONa(aq) + H_2O(l)$$

SAQ 6.4

Write balanced equations for the reactions of:

a zinc with propanoic acid;

b sodium carbonate with methanoic acid;

c magnesium oxide with ethanoic acid;

d benzoic acid with sodium hydroxide.

● **Figure 6.4** The concentration of ethanoic acid in vinegar may be found by titration.

You can titrate ethanoic acid, or wine that has been oxidised to vinegar, against sodium hydroxide to determine the concentration of acid present *(figure 6.4)*. Vinegar is between 6% and 10% ethanoic acid. As ethanoic acid is a weak acid, an indicator for the titration of a strong base against a weak acid is required (such as phenolphthalein).

Formation of esters

The formation of an ester from a carboxylic acid is known as **esterification**. You can prepare ethyl ethanoate by warming a mixture of ethanol and glacial ethanoic acid in the presence of concentrated sulphuric acid as a catalyst. (Glacial ethanoic acid is pure ethanoic acid, free of water. It is called glacial because it freezes in the bottle at $16.7\,°C$ *(figure 6.5)*.) The equation for the formation of ethyl ethanoate is:

$$H_3C-C{\overset{O}{\underset{O-H}{\Vert}}} + CH_3CH_2OH \rightleftharpoons H_3C-C{\overset{O}{\underset{O-CH_2CH_3}{\Vert}}} + H_2O$$

ethyl ethanoate

You can make esters of aliphatic alcohols in this way. You will need to use acyl chlorides or anhydrides to make esters of aromatic alcohols (see pages 68 and 69).

● **Figure 6.5** Glacial ethanoic acid freezes at $16.7\,°C$.

Formation of acyl chlorides

In chapter 4, we saw that phosphorus(V) chloride was useful in testing for the presence of the hydroxyl group in alcohols. An alkyl chloride is formed and misty fumes of hydrogen chloride are evolved. Phosphorus(V) chloride also produces misty fumes of hydrogen chloride when reacted with a carboxylic acid. The organic product is an acyl chloride.

The reaction of benzoic acid with phosphorus(V) chloride produces benzoyl chloride:

benzoyl chloride

Both benzoic acid and phosphorus(V) chloride are solids. Benzoyl chloride is a liquid. If you mix and shake the two solids you will see them liquefy slowly and give off misty fumes of hydrogen chloride. Oxyphosphorus(V) chloride is the third product.

SAQ 6.5

Write balanced equations for the reaction of propanoic acid with:

a methanol; **b** phosphorus(V) chloride.

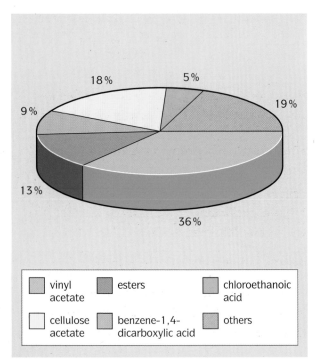

● **Figure 6.6** The major uses of ethanoic acid.

The uses of ethanoic acid

These are shown in *figure 6.6*. Ethenyl ethanoate, $CH_3COOCH=CH_2$, (formerly known as vinyl acetate) is used to make the polymer poly(ethenyl ethanoate) (formerly polyvinyl acetate). Benzene-1,4-dicarboxylic acid is used to make polyester (page 87). Cellulose ethanoate (cellulose acetate) is used as a synthetic fibre and the transparent sheet for photographic film. Chloroethanoic acid is used to make the selective herbicide 2,4-D, used to kill broad-leaved weeds in grass.

Acyl chlorides

The structure of the acyl chloride functional group is:

The general formula for a member of the homologous series of acyl chlorides is $C_nH_{2n+1}COCl$, where $n = 0$, 1, 2 etc. Like nitriles and carboxylic acids, the carbon atom in the functional group, $-COCl$, is included in the count of carbon atoms. Acyl chlorides are named systematically from the parent alkane by replacing the final '-e' with '-oyl chloride'. So CH_3CH_2COCl is named propanoyl chloride.

The reactions of acyl chlorides

Acyl chlorides form a group of very reactive compounds that may be used to join an alkanoyl group RCO– onto an alcohol, phenol or amine. (In view of the highly exothermic nature of acyl chloride reactions, the chemical process industry often uses an acid anhydride instead to achieve the same end. Acid anhydrides release less heat energy on reaction, cost less than acyl chlorides and do not release hydrogen chloride on reaction. For example, ethanoic anhydride

is used to make aspirin and cellulose ethanoate.)

Hydrolysis

Ethanoyl chloride is immiscible with water. However, when a few drops of ethanoyl chloride are added to water in a test tube, a violent, exothermic reaction occurs, misty fumes are evolved and the resulting solution smells of vinegar. The equation for the reaction is:

$$CH_3COCl(l) + H_2O(l)$$
$$\longrightarrow CH_3COOH(aq) + HCl(g)$$

The fumes of hydrogen chloride produce a dense white smoke of ammonium chloride if they pass over a drop of concentrated ammonia (*figure 6.7*). Alternatively, they will turn a drop of silver nitrate milky. The rapid hydrolysis of ethanoyl chloride is in marked contrast to the much slower rate of hydrolysis of chloroalkanes in general. You may recall that the rate of hydrolysis depends on the nature of the hydrocarbon (see page 41). In fact, chlorobenzene does not react with water at all, even when heated. Acyl halides are hydrolysed much more rapidly because the reaction proceeds by a different mechanism. This is because of the presence of the carbonyl group. Nucleophilic addition of a water molecule across the very polar carbonyl group is followed by elimination of hydrogen chloride.

● **Figure 6.7** Ethanoyl chloride reacts with water to produce fumes of hydrogen chloride, which can be tested using a drop of aqueous ammonia on a glass rod.

Reactions with alcohols and phenols

Alcohols and phenols also behave as nucleophiles. They react with acyl chlorides to form esters. In chapter 4, we saw how esters could be made from alcohols and carboxylic acids in the presence of an acid catalyst. However, phenols with carboxylic acids do not readily form esters.

If you add ethanoyl chloride dropwise to ethanol, the liquid boils violently and fumes of hydrogen chloride are evolved. An oily product smelling of pears remains. This product is ethyl ethanoate and the equation for the reaction is:

$$H_3C-\overset{\displaystyle O}{\underset{\displaystyle Cl}{C}}\text{(l)} + CH_3CH_2OH(l) \rightarrow H_3C-\overset{\displaystyle O}{\underset{\displaystyle O-CH_2CH_3}{C}}\text{(l)} + HCl(g)$$

ethyl ethanoate

Ethyl ethanoate is a volatile liquid and hence can be purified by distillation.

The ester phenyl benzoate may be prepared by dissolving phenol in aqueous sodium hydroxide and shaking with benzoyl chloride. The overall reaction is:

benzoyl chloride

phenyl benzoate

Phenyl benzoate is a solid which is purified by recrystallisation (page 12) using methylated spirit.

Reaction with primary amines

When reacted with amines, acyl chlorides produce amides. Ethanoyl chloride reacts with ethylamine to produce the amide $CH_3CONHCH_2CH_3$. The equation for the reaction is:

$$H_3C-\overset{\displaystyle O}{\underset{\displaystyle Cl}{C}} + CH_3CH_2NH_2 \longrightarrow H_3C-\overset{\displaystyle O}{\underset{\displaystyle NHCH_2CH_3}{C}} + HCl$$

Hydrogen chloride is neutralised by excess amine as it is formed (page 78). The amide functional group (see chapter 7) is:

SAQ 6.6

Write balanced equations for the reactions of propanoyl chloride with:

a water;

b methanol;

c ethylamine.

Esters

The ester functional group is:

$$-C{\overset{O}{\underset{O-C}{\big\|}}}$$

Esters are formed by the reaction of an alcohol with a carboxylic acid (chapter 4) or by the reaction of an alcohol or a phenol with an acyl chloride (page 69).

The name of an ester comes partly from the parent alcohol and partly from the parent acid. The alcohol part of the name is placed first and is separated by a space before the acid part of the name. An example is ethyl propanoate:

$$CH_3CH_2-O-\overset{O}{\underset{}{\overset{\|}{C}}}-CH_2CH_3$$

ethyl — propanoate

A range of isomers may be formulated by moving carbon atoms from one side of the ester group to the other. Ethyl propanoate has methyl butanoate, propyl ethanoate and butyl methanoate as isomers (all of which are esters).

SAQ 6.7

a Draw structural formulae for those isomers of ethyl propanoate that are constructed by moving carbon atoms from one side of the ester group to the other.

b Further isomers with the same molecular formula as ethyl propanoate are possible, not all of which are esters. Draw the structural formulae of as many of these as you can and name them.

The hydrolysis of esters

Esters may be hydrolysed by refluxing with either an acid or an alkali. Refluxing with an acid simply reverses the preparation of the ester from an alcohol and a carboxylic acid. The acid catalyses the reaction. The reaction is an equilibrium; hence there are always molecules of both reactants and products present after the reaction. The equation for the acid hydrolysis of ethyl ethanoate is:

$$H_3C-C{\overset{O}{\underset{O-CH_2CH_3}{\big\|}}} + H_2O \underset{}{\overset{H^+(aq)}{\rightleftharpoons}} H_3C-C{\overset{O}{\underset{O-H}{\big\|}}} + CH_3CH_2OH$$

When an ester is refluxed with an alkali such as aqueous sodium hydroxide, it is fully hydrolysed to the alcohol and the sodium salt of the acid. The equation for the base hydrolysis of ethyl ethanoate is:

$$H_3C-C{\overset{O}{\underset{O-CH_2CH_3}{\big\|}}} + OH^- \longrightarrow H_3C-C{\overset{O}{\underset{O^-}{\big\|}}} + CH_3CH_2OH$$

When the ester is a benzoate, base hydrolysis with aqueous sodium hydroxide produces an aqueous solution of sodium benzoate. Subsequent acidification produces a white precipitate of benzoic acid, as benzoic acid is only sparingly soluble in water (*figure 6.8*).

SAQ 6.8

a Write a balanced equation for the base hydrolysis of methyl benzoate.

b Write a balanced equation for the acid hydrolysis of methyl propanoate.

● *Figure 6.8* Benzoic acid precipitates when sodium benzoate is acidified.

Fats as natural esters

Vegetable oils and animal fats provide an important store of energy for plants and animals. Oils and fats are esters of propane-1,2,3-triol. This alcohol has three hydroxyl groups, each of which can form an ester when reacted with a carboxylic acid. When only *one* of the alcohol groups has been esterified, the product is called a **monoglyceride**. In **diglycerides**, any *two* of the alcohol groups have been esterified. **Triglycerides** have had all *three* alcohol groups esterified. You can use different carboxylic acids to esterify each of the hydroxyl groups. *Table 6.2* (page 66) shows a few of the carboxylic acids which form these esters. *Figure 6.9* shows a molecular model of a triglyceride.

We shall look more closely at the structure of one triglyceride containing the fatty acid octadecanoic acid (stearic acid). The structures of propane-1,2,3-triol and octadecanoic acid are:

$$CH_2OH$$
$$|$$
$$CHOH$$
$$|$$
$$CH_2OH$$

propane-1,2,3-triol
glycerol

$$\overset{O}{\underset{HO}{\overset{\|}{C}}} - (CH_2)_{16}CH_3$$

octadecanoic acid
stearic acid

The triglyceride formed from three moles of octadecanoic acid and one mole of propane-1,2,3-triol is:

$$H_3C(H_2C)_{16} - \overset{O}{\overset{\|}{C}} - O - \overset{\overset{\displaystyle H_2C - O - \overset{O}{\overset{\|}{C}} - (CH_2)_{16}CH_3}{|}}{\underset{\underset{\displaystyle H_2C - O - \overset{O}{\overset{\|}{C}} - (CH_2)_{16}CH_3}{|}}{CH}}$$

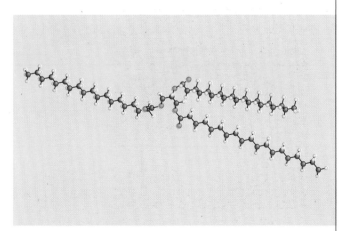

● *Figure 6.9* A triglyceride.

SAQ 6.9

a What is the other product when octadecanoic acid and propane-1,2,3-triol form a triglyceride?

b What type of reaction has taken place?

c How many moles of this second product are formed per mole of propane-1,2,3-triol?

d Write a balanced equation for the reaction using structural formulae.

Fats and oils can be hydrolysed (like other esters) by heating with an acid or a base. When they are refluxed with sodium hydroxide, they are converted into propane-1,2,3-triol and the sodium salts of the fatty acids present. These sodium salts of fatty acids are soaps, so this hydrolysis is known as a **saponification**, meaning 'the forming of soap' (from *sapo*, the Latin word for soap). The reaction forms the basis of our modern soap-making industry. Soap making has been known to humans for many thousands of years. Soap is described in the Bible (Jeremiah 2:22). In the first century AD, the Roman historian Pliny described a method of soap manufacture that used goats' fat and beechwood ashes.

The equation for the saponification of the triglyceride prepared from propane-1,2,3-triol and octadecanoic acid is given in *figure 6.10a*. After the saponification process, the soap is present in solution. It is precipitated as a solid by adding an excess of sodium chloride to the reaction mixture – a process known as **salting out**. Modern soaps (*figure 6.10b*) are made from blends of oils to produce particular combinations of properties.

The uses of esters

Significant quantities of esters are used as solvents in the chemical industry and as adhesives. Nail varnish (or its remover) and whiteboard marker pens may contain ethyl ethanoate as a solvent.

The flavours and fragrances of different esters are widely used to produce food flavourings and perfumes. The natural flavours of fruits are the result of subtle blends of hundreds of organic compounds. Many of these compounds are esters of aliphatic alcohols and simple carboxylic acids.

● *Figure 6.11* Oil of jasmine is a natural oil used in perfumes. It used to be obtained from the jasmine plant, but now it is manufactured using phenylmethanol and ethanoic acid.

● *Figure 6.10*

a The saponification reaction produces soap.

b A noodling machine, part of the soap-making process.

cheaply and readily available. Oil of jasmine is phenylmethyl ethanoate:

The perfume industry now relies heavily on chemical synthesis to provide the basic fragrances for many expensive perfumes.

In this context, we have already mentioned ethyl 2-methylbutanoate and 3-methylbutyl ethanoate. *Table 6.4* shows a number of esters with their approximate associated flavours and their molecular models.

The fragrance of a flower or plant is produced by volatile organic compounds. These may be extracted as the 'essential oil' of the flower or plant. These essential oils are the basis of the perfume industry; they contain a variety of compounds such as esters, aldehydes, terpenes and phenols. (The distinguishing feature of terpenes is that they are built up from a common five-carbon-atom unit based on 2-methylbuta-1,3-diene (isoprene), page 25.) Oil of jasmine (*figure 6.11*), traditionally obtained from the plant jasmine, is now produced by chemical synthesis and is thus

Flavour	*Esters*	*Molecular model*
apple	ethyl 2-methylbutanoate	
pear	3-methylbutyl ethanoate	
banana	1-methylbutyl ethanoate	
pineapple	butyl butanoate	

● *Table 6.4* Some esters and their associated flavours

SUMMARY

■ The carboxylic acid functional group is –COOH. Carboxylic acids are found naturally in many foods. The systematic name for a carboxylic acid derives from the name of the alkane, with the '-e' replaced by '-oic acid'.

■ Esters are formed when carboxylic acids react with alcohols. A water molecule is released in the reaction. The ester functional group is –COOC–. Esters of aliphatic alcohols have fruity odours and are principal components of the flavours of many fruits. Fats and oils are esters of propane-1,2,3-triol (glycerol) and long-chain carboxylic acids.

■ Acyl chlorides contain the –COCl functional group.

■ Carboxylic acids may be made by oxidation of primary alcohols or by hydrolysing a nitrile. Industrially, they are obtained from fats or by the oxidation of a petroleum feedstock. Carboxylic acids may be reduced to primary alcohols (via aldehydes) using lithium tetrahydridoaluminate.

■ The polar carbonyl group is responsible for the acidic behaviour of carboxylic acids. They readily form salts with alkalis, bases or carbonates. Acid strength is increased by the presence of halogen atoms on the carbon atom attached to the –COOH group.

■ Esters form when an aliphatic alcohol and a carboxylic acid are warmed in the presence of an acid catalyst. Acyl chlorides form when carboxylic acids are treated with phosphorus(V) chloride.

■ Acyl chlorides are hydrolysed to carboxylic acids by water, form esters with alcohols or phenols and form amides with ammonia or amines.

■ Esters are hydrolysed to form alcohols and carboxylic acids by warming the ester with an acid catalyst. Warming an ester with an alkali produces an alcohol and a carboxylic acid salt. Alkaline hydrolysis of a fat or oil produces propane-1,2,3-triol and the salt of a fatty acid. These salts are soaps, so the hydrolysis of a fat or oil is often called saponification.

■ Esters are used as flavours and fragrances. Apart from its use in vinegar, ethanoic acid is an important feedstock for the chemical industry.

Questions

1 The compound shown below is ibuprofen, a powerful painkiller that is much less likely than paracetamol to cause liver damage through overdose.

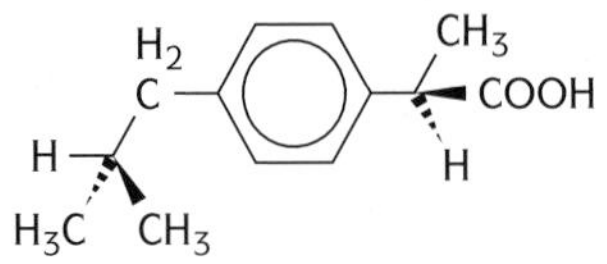

a Copy the structure of ibuprofen and draw a circle round any chiral centre in the molecule.

b Calculate the relative molecular mass of ibuprofen.

c Ibuprofen is sold in tablet form, with each tablet containing 300 mg of the compound. How many tablets would you need to make one mole of the compound?

d Under certain conditions, ibuprofen reacts with ethanol and a pleasant smelling product is formed.
  (i) Suggest the conditions needed for this reaction to occur.
  (ii) Give a balanced equation for the reaction.

e Describe what you would observe when ibuprofen is treated with phosphorus(V) chloride. Give a balanced equation for the reaction.

2 On hydrolysis with aqueous sodium hydroxide, a sample of oil (an ester) produced the sodium salts of the following acids:
  K: $CH_3(CH_2)_{14}CO_2H$
  L: $CH_3(CH_2)_7CH=CH(CH_2)_7CO_2H$;
  M: $CH_3(CH_2)_{16}CO_2H$.

a What is the other organic product of this hydrolysis?

b Draw a diagram of the structure of the oil, showing clearly how the oxygen atoms are bonded.

c Acid L exists as *cis–trans* isomers. Draw diagrams to illustrate this type of isomerism.

d Starting with ethene as the only carbon-containing compound, outline how you would obtain a reasonably pure sample of ethyl ethanoate. Your reaction scheme should include any other reagents and an indication of the reaction conditions.

e A compound N, $C_4H_8O_2$, does not react with phosphorus(V) chloride but, on warming with aqueous sodium hydroxide followed by acidification, forms two organic products, P and Q. Oxidation of P with acidified potassium dichromate(VI) produces a compound R with molecular formula $C_2H_4O_2$, which gives off carbon dioxide when it is reacted with sodium carbonate. Identify N, P, Q and R, explaining your reasoning and the purpose of each of the tests described.

Nitrogen compounds

1 describe the formation of ethylamine by nitrile reduction and of phenylamine by the reduction of nitro-benzene;

2 explain the basicity of amines;

3 explain the relative basicities of ammonia, ethylamine and phenylamine in terms of their structures;

4 describe the reactions of phenylamine with bromine and with nitrous acid;

5 describe the coupling of benzenediazonium chloride and phenol, and the use of similar reactions in the formation of dyestuffs;

6 describe the formation of amides from amines and acyl chlorides;

7 describe amide hydrolysis on treatment with aqueous alkali or acid;

8 describe the acid/base properties of amino acids and the formation of zwitterions.

Nitrogen may be present in an organic molecule in a number of functional groups.

■ The amine functional group, $-NH_2$, occurs in a wide variety of compounds. These range from simple amines to medicines, dyes and giant biological macromolecules. The smell given off by rotting animal flesh is largely caused by amines such as putrescine, $NH_2(CH_2)_4NH_2$, and cadaverine, $NH_2(CH_2)_5NH_2$. Urea, present in urine, has the structure:

$$O = C \begin{cases} NH_2 \\ NH_2 \end{cases}$$

Amphetamine is a medicine used as a stimulant that mimics the effect of noradrenaline. Noradrenaline is a neurotransmitter that prepares animals for a rapid response when, for example, they are suddenly frightened *(figure 7.1)*. Noradrenaline and amphetamine increase the heart rate, dilate the air passages in the lungs

● *Figure 7.1* When springbok are frightened they will take flight, frequently leaping high into the air (an activity known as 'pronking'). The rapid response is triggered by a release of noradrenaline.

and increase sweating. They have similar structures:

noradrenaline (norepinephrine)   amphetamine

The double helix present in DNA is held together by hydrogen bonds between pairs of bases *(figure 7.2)*. Amine functional groups are involved in some of these hydrogen bonds. The hydrogen bonds between the cytosine and guanine bases are shown in *figure 7.2b*. Amino acids also contain the amine group. For example:

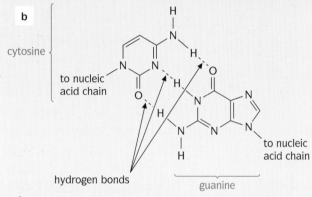

Figure 7.2 **a** Watson and Crick with their first model of DNA. **b** Hydrogen bonds between a base pair in DNA.

SAQ 7.1

Copy the diagram of hydrogen bonds between the cytosine and guanine bases. Draw circles round the amine functional groups and label them.

■ The amide functional group, –CONH–, is present in proteins and polyamides. Some synthetic polymers, such as nylon, are polyamides. The repeat units of a protein and a polyamide are:

repeat unit of a protein

repeat unit of a polyamide

SAQ 7.2

Copy the repeat units of a protein and a polyamide. Draw circles round the amide functional groups and label them.

■ The nitrile functional group, –CN, (see also chapters 3, 5 and 6) is used to introduce an additional carbon atom during organic synthesis. However, it is also present in the synthetic polymer used to make acrylic fibre. Poly(ethenenitrile) (also called polyacrylonitrile) is made by polymerising ethenenitrile:

This polymer is used to make acrylic fibre, which is widely used for clothing and furnishing fabrics. It is an interesting thought that when we wear acrylic garments *(figure 7.3)*, we cover ourselves in cyanide (nitrile) groups. Sodium cyanide and hydrogen cyanide are highly toxic but, fortunately, the cyanide groups in acrylic fabric are firmly bonded in the polymer, and represent no danger. However, a hazard can arise if the material is burned and the fumes are inhaled. As a result, modern acrylic fibre is modified by the inclusion of some chloroethene. The chlorine atoms provide a substantially increased resistance to combustion.

Figure 7.3 Acrylics are used in clothing and furnishing materials.

Primary amines

The primary amines which we shall study in detail are ethylamine and phenylamine. Models of their structures are shown in *figure 7.4*. Primary aliphatic amines are generally water-soluble. The hydrogen atoms in the amine group, $-NH_2$, form hydrogen bonds to the oxygen atoms in the water molecules. A hydrogen atom in water may also hydrogen-bond to the nitrogen of the amino group *(figure 7.5)*. The solubility in water of the primary aliphatic amines reduces as the number of carbon atoms in the alkyl group increases. Alkyl groups are non-polar and can only form weak, instantaneous dipole-induced bonds to other molecules. The breaking of these bonds provides insufficient energy to disrupt the much stronger hydrogen bonding between water molecules. (Phenylamine also has a low solubility in water, for the same reason.)

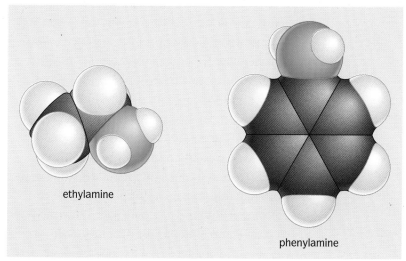

ethylamine

phenylamine

● *Figure 7.4* Amines.

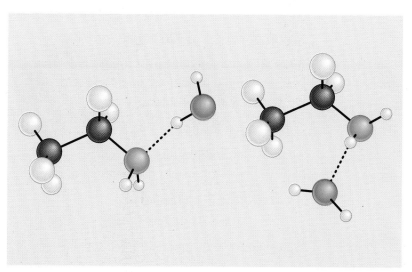

● *Figure 7.5* The formation of hydrogen bonds between water and ethylamine.

The preparation of amines

Here are two methods for preparing ethylamine.

- Heating bromoethane with a hot, alcoholic solution of ammonia under pressure produces ethylamine:

$$CH_3CH_2Br + NH_3 \longrightarrow CH_3CH_2NH_2 + HBr$$

We discussed this reaction in detail in chapter 3 (page 41).

- Reducing ethanenitrile with hydrogen produces ethylamine:

$$CH_3CN + 4[H] \longrightarrow CH_3CH_2NH_2$$

The hydrogen may come from lithium tetrahydridoaluminate, sodium in ethanol, or hydrogen gas with nickel. We discussed the reduction of a nitrile to an amine in detail in chapter 5 (page 60).

Phenylamine is prepared by reducing nitrobenzene:

$$\text{⬡}-NO_2 + 6[H]$$

$$\downarrow$$

$$\text{⬡}-NH_2 + 2H_2O$$

The reduction is carried out using tin in hydrochloric acid. The product is separated from the reaction mixture by steam distillation, which involves distilling the mixture whilst passing steam through the mixture *(figure 7.6)*. Arenes are readily nitrated, so the reduction of nitroarenes provides a standard route to aromatic amines.

● **Figure 7.6** This student is carrying out a steam distillation.

SAQ 7.3

Give the name and structural formula of the organic product from the reactions of:

a propanenitrile with hydrogen and a nickel catalyst;

b 4-nitrophenol with tin and hydrochloric acid.

Amines as bases

Amines are related to ammonia, which is a weak base. Weak bases will accept a proton from water to form an alkaline solution. The equation for the reaction of ammonia with water is:

$$H - \overset{\cdot\cdot}{\underset{H}{N}} - H + H_2O \longrightarrow \left[H - \overset{\overset{H}{\uparrow}}{\underset{H}{N}} - H \right]^{+} + OH^{-}$$

Ammonia has a lone-pair of electrons on the nitrogen atom. This lone-pair accepts a proton from a water molecule to form the ammonium ion. A mixture of ammonia and ammonium ions is present in an aqueous solution of ammonia. If we represent a general amine by the formula RNH_2, the general equation for the reaction with water is:

$$RNH_2(aq) + H_2O(l) \rightleftharpoons RNH_3^{+}(aq) + OH^{-}(aq)$$

For example, ethylamine accepts a proton to form the ethylammonium ion:

$$H_3C - \overset{}{\underset{H_2}{C}} - \overset{\cdot\cdot}{\underset{H}{N}} - H + H_2O \longrightarrow \left[H_3C - \overset{}{\underset{H_2}{C}} - \overset{\overset{H}{\uparrow}}{\underset{H}{N}} - H \right]^{+} + OH^{-}$$

Amine	pK_b	Order of base strength
phenylamine	9.3	
ammonia	4.7	increasing strength
ethylamine	3.3	

● **Table 7.1** Base strengths of amines and ammonia

The base strengths of ethylamine and phenylamine relative to ammonia are shown in *table 7.1*. The quantity pK_b is a measure of the base strength. The smaller this value, the stronger the base strength. The order of base strength is due to the inductive effects of the ethyl and phenyl groups.

■ Alkyl groups have a positive inductive effect. This means that they have a tendency to push electrons towards a neighbouring atom. In ethylamine, the effect of this is to increase slightly the electron charge density on the nitrogen atom. This increased charge density on the nitrogen atom enhances its ability to donate its lone-pair of electrons to a proton, so ethylamine is a stronger base than ammonia.

■ The phenyl group has a negative inductive effect. The electron charge density on the nitrogen atom in phenylamine is decreased. Consequently, the ability of phenylamine to accept a proton is decreased, so it is a weaker base than ammonia. This effect is further enhanced in phenylamine because the lone-pair of electrons on the nitrogen atom becomes partially delocalised over the benzene ring.

Making salts with amines

Bases are neutralised by acids to form salts. For example, ammonia with hydrochloric acid produces ammonium chloride:

$$NH_3(aq) + HCl(aq) \longrightarrow NH_4^{+}(aq) + Cl^{-}(aq)$$

Amines also produce salts. Ethylamine with hydrochloric acid forms ethylammonium chloride:

$$C_2H_5NH_2(aq) + HCl(aq)$$
$$\longrightarrow C_2H_5NH_3^{+}(aq) + Cl^{-}(aq)$$

Phenylamine forms phenylammonium chloride:

$$\langle\text{benzene ring}\rangle - NH_2 + HCl \longrightarrow \langle\text{benzene ring}\rangle - NH_3^{+}Cl^{-}$$

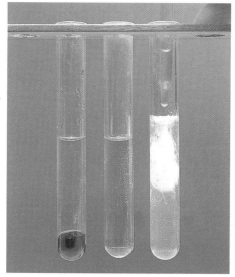

● **Figure 7.7** The left-hand tube contains brown phenyl-amine, which does not mix with water. The central tube contains a solution of phenylamine in acid. A white emulsion forms when alkali is added to this solution.

Phenylamine is only sparingly soluble in water, but it dissolves readily in hydrochloric acid because a salt is formed. Addition of alkali to this salt solution causes phenylamine to be released. Initially, a milky emulsion forms, which usually breaks down into oily drops (*figure 7.7*). (Compare this to the behaviour of a solution of phenol in aqueous alkali on treatment with hydrochloric acid (page 52).)

SAQ 7.4

Write balanced equations for the reactions of:

a nitric acid with butylamine;

b hydrochloric acid with 4-aminophenol;

c sodium hydroxide with 4-aminophenol.

Reactions specific to phenylamine

Diazonium salt formation and coupling reactions

Amines react with nitrous acid to produce nitrogen gas and a variety of organic products. For example, ethylamine produces a mixture which includes ethanol and ethene, and phenylamine produces phenol and nitrogen on warming with nitrous acid:

$$\text{C}_6\text{H}_5\text{—NH}_2 + \text{HNO}_2 \longrightarrow \text{C}_6\text{H}_5\text{—OH} + \text{N}_2 + \text{H}_2\text{O}$$

(The nitrous acid needed for these reactions is unstable and is produced by reacting sodium nitrite with dilute hydrochloric acid.)

However, if the reaction mixture of phenylamine and nitrous acid is kept below 5 °C, a diazonium salt is formed (the azo group is –N=N–). This reaction is known as a **diazotisation** reaction:

$$\text{C}_6\text{H}_5\text{—NH}_2 + \text{HNO}_2 + \text{HCl} \rightarrow \text{C}_6\text{H}_5\text{—N}^{\oplus}\equiv\text{NCl}^{\ominus} + 2\text{H}_2\text{O}$$

phenyldiazonium chloride

The diazonium group, $-\text{N}_2^+$, is rather unstable and decomposes readily to nitrogen. However, delocalisation of the diazonium π-bond electrons over a benzene ring stabilises phenyldiazonium sufficiently for it to form at low temperatures.

The phenyldiazonium behaves as an electrophile, and will attack another arene molecule such as phenol. Electrophilic substitution takes place at the 4 position, producing 4-hydroxy-phenylazobenzene (*figure 7.8*). The reaction is known as a **coupling** reaction:

$$\text{C}_6\text{H}_5\text{—N}_2^+ + \text{C}_6\text{H}_5\text{—OH} \rightarrow \text{C}_6\text{H}_5\text{—N}=\text{N—C}_6\text{H}_4\text{—OH} + \text{H}^+$$

The compound formed is an energetically stable, yellow azo dye. The stability is due to extensive

● **Figure 7.8** A diazonium dye is formed when phenyl-diazonium chloride is added to phenol.

delocalisation of the electrons via the nitrogen–nitrogen double bond. If you examine the structure of the product you can see how double and single bonds alternate. Systems of alternating double and single bonds are called **conjugated** systems. Where extensive conjugation occurs, absorption of visible light takes place so the compound is coloured. A very different conjugated system to that in 4-hydroxyphenylazobenzene is present in carotene. Carotene is bright orange and occurs in carrots, for example. It has the structure:

The conjugated system that is responsible for the light absorption is known as a **chromophore**. (The conjugated system in benzene also absorbs electromagnetic radiation. However, it only absorbs at higher energy in the ultraviolet region, so benzene is colourless.)

The dye 4-hydroxyphenylazobenzene is just one of the wide range of dyes that can be made from aromatic amines and other arenes. These are known as diazonium dyes. They are very stable, so they do not fade. Another example is the indicator methyl orange (*figure 7.9*) which has the structure:

$Na^{\oplus}{}^{\ominus}O_3S$ —〈benzene ring〉— $N=N$ —〈benzene ring〉— $N\begin{smallmatrix}CH_3\\CH_3\end{smallmatrix}$

● **Figure 7.9** Methyl orange is used as an indicator.

SAQ 7.5

Draw the displayed formula for the azo dye produced on reacting 4-aminophenol with nitrous acid (in dilute hydrochloric acid) below 5°C and coupling the resulting diazonium salt with phenol. Write balanced equations for the reactions involved.

Substitution by bromine

When we discussed amines as bases, we saw that the lone-pair of electrons on the nitrogen atom in phenylamine was partly delocalised over the benzene ring. This has the effect of enriching the electron charge density on the benzene ring at the 2, 4 and 6 positions. This enrichment of electron charge makes phenylamine much more reactive than benzene towards electrophiles such as bromine. (Benzene requires an iron(III) bromide catalyst and liquid bromine to produce the monosubstituted bromobenzene.) Phenylamine produces the trisubstituted 2,4,6-tribromophenylamine when reacted with aqueous bromine and no catalyst (*figure 7.10*):

$$\text{〈}C_6H_5NH_2\text{〉} + 3Br_2 \longrightarrow \text{〈}2,4,6\text{-tribromophenylamine〉} + 3HBr$$

Compare this product to that produced by the reaction of phenol with aqueous bromine (page 53).

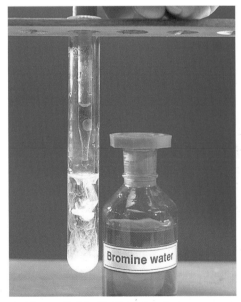

● **Figure 7.10** The reaction that occurs when bromine water is added to aqueous phenylamine.

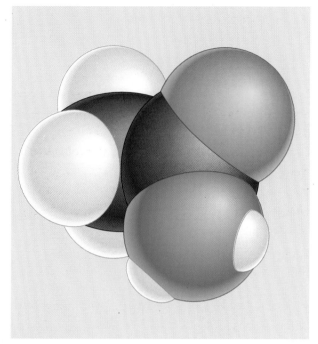

● *Figure 7.11* Ethanamide.

Amides

Figure 7.11 shows the structure and a molecular model of ethanamide. Ethanamide is made by adding ethanoyl chloride dropwise to ammonia (dropwise addition is essential as the reaction is violent):

$$H_3C - C{\small\begin{matrix}O\\Cl\end{matrix}} + H - N{\small\begin{matrix}H\\H\end{matrix}} \longrightarrow H_3C - C{\small\begin{matrix}O\\NH_2\end{matrix}} + HCl$$

Ethanoic anhydride may be used instead of ethanoyl chloride.

Ethanamide is a primary amide. Reaction of a primary amine with ethanoyl chloride produces a secondary amide. The equation for the reaction is:

$$H_3C - C{\small\begin{matrix}O\\Cl\end{matrix}} + H - N{\small\begin{matrix}R\\H\end{matrix}} \longrightarrow H_3C - C{\small\begin{matrix}O\\NHR\end{matrix}} + HCl$$

where R– represents an alkyl group, such as the ethyl group.

Hydrolysis of amides

Amide hydrolysis is catalysed by acid or alkali.

■ Refluxing a primary amide with alkali releases ammonia, and leaves a carboxylate ion in solution. During hydrolysis, the C–N bond is broken. The equation for the alkaline hydrolysis of ethanamide is:

$$H_3C - C{\small\begin{matrix}O\\NH_2\end{matrix}} + OH^- \longrightarrow H_3C - C{\small\begin{matrix}O\\O^\ominus\end{matrix}} + NH_3$$

■ Acid hydrolysis of a primary amide produces a carboxylic acid and ammonium ions. The equation for the acidic hydrolysis of ethanamide is:

$$H_3C - C{\small\begin{matrix}O\\NH_2\end{matrix}} + H^+ + H_2O \longrightarrow H_3C - C{\small\begin{matrix}O\\OH\end{matrix}} + NH_4^+$$

Compare the hydrolysis of amides with the hydrolysis of esters (page 70). Note also that the hydrolysis of polypeptides and proteins to form amino acids also involves breaking the C–N bond in the amide (peptide) links (see chapter 8).

SAQ 7.6

Name and draw the structural formulae for:

a all the possible products when ethanoyl chloride is added to 4-aminophenol;

b the products formed in the acid hydrolysis of propanamide.

Amino acids

There are about twenty naturally occurring amino acids. The general structure of these amino acids is:

$$R - \underset{\underset{COOH}{|}}{\overset{\overset{NH_2}{|}}{C}} - H$$

They are all α-**amino acids**, which have the amino group and the carboxylic acid group attached to the same carbon atom. In the simplest amino acid, glycine, the 'R' is a hydrogen atom. In the next simplest amino acid, alanine, the 'R' is a methyl group, CH_3.

Amino acids are **bifunctional**, that is they have two functional groups present in the molecule: the carboxylic acid group, $-COOH$, and the amino group, $-NH_2$. As one of these groups is acidic and the other group is basic, they can interact with one another. The $-COOH$ group donates a proton to the $-NH_2$ group. This forms an 'internal' salt known as a **zwitterion**:

$$R-\underset{\underset{\text{COOH}}{|}}{\overset{\overset{\text{NH}_2}{|}}{C}}-H \longrightarrow R-\underset{\underset{\text{COO}^\ominus}{|}}{\overset{\overset{\overset{\oplus}{\text{NH}_3}}{|}}{C}}-H$$

a zwitterion

The zwitterion has a significant effect on the properties of amino acids. It is the predominant form of the amino acid in the solid phase or in aqueous solution. The ionic charges increase the attractive forces between the amino acids in the solid, and so raise the melting point significantly above that of related compounds with similar numbers of atoms and electrons. The amino acid glycine, NH_2CH_2COOH, decomposes at $262\,^\circ C$ without melting, whereas propanoic acid, CH_3CH_2COOH, melts at $-21\,^\circ C$.

Amino acids form salts when reacted with acids or bases. On addition of a dilute solution of a strong acid (for example, aqueous hydrochloric acid), the zwitterion will accept a proton. The product now carries a net positive charge and may be crystallised as the chloride salt:

$$R-\underset{\underset{\text{COO}^\ominus}{|}}{\overset{\overset{\overset{\oplus}{\text{NH}_3}}{|}}{C}}-H + H^+ \longrightarrow R-\underset{\underset{\text{COOH}}{|}}{\overset{\overset{\overset{\oplus}{\text{NH}_3}}{|}}{C}}-H$$

Addition of dilute aqueous sodium hydroxide removes the proton from the $-NH_3{}^+$ group in the zwitterion. This leaves a negatively charged ion:

$$R-\underset{\underset{\text{COO}^\ominus}{|}}{\overset{\overset{\overset{\oplus}{\text{NH}_3}}{|}}{C}}-H + OH^- \longrightarrow R-\underset{\underset{\text{COO}^\ominus}{|}}{\overset{\overset{\text{NH}_2}{|}}{C}}-H + H_2O$$

Hence at high pH, amino acids are negatively charged in aqueous solution. At low pH, they are positively charged.

SAQ 7.7

a Draw the structural formulae for the ions present when glycine, NH_2CH_2COOH, is dissolved in:

(i) aqueous hydrochloric acid;

(ii) aqueous sodium hydroxide.

b Write balanced equations for the reaction of aqueous glycine with:

(i) aqueous hydrochloric acid;

(ii) aqueous sodium hydroxide.

Optical isomerism in amino acids

With the exception of glycine, amino acids have four different groups round the α carbon atom. This constitutes a chiral centre, and optical isomers are possible. The mirror images of the optical isomers of alanine may be drawn using three-dimensional formulae, as follows:

mirror plane

When you need to represent a pair of optical isomers, draw one isomer using the three-dimensional representation. Next, imagine reflecting this isomer in a mirror plane, and draw the other isomer.

SAQ 7.8

a Leucine has the structure:

$$H_2N-\underset{\underset{\underset{\text{CH(CH}_3)_2}{|}}{\overset{|}{\text{CH}_2}}}{\overset{\overset{\text{H}}{|}}{C}}-COOH$$

Draw three-dimensional formulae to show the optical isomers of leucine.

b Isoleucine has more than one chiral centre. It has the structure:

$$H_2N-\underset{\underset{\underset{\text{CH}_3}{|}}{\overset{|}{\text{CHCH}_2\text{CH}_3}}}{\overset{\overset{\text{H}}{|}}{C}}-COOH$$

Copy this structure and mark the chiral centres with asterisks.

SUMMARY

■ Nitrogen appears in organic compounds in the following functional groups: amine, $-NH_2$; amide, $-CONH_2$; nitrile, $-CN$; and azo, $-N=N-$. Such groups are common amongst the biochemical molecules found in living things.

■ Ethylamine is prepared either by treating bromoethane with hot, alcoholic ammonia under pressure or by reducing ethanenitrile. Phenylamine is prepared by reducing nitrobenzene using tin and hydrochloric acid.

■ Like ammonia, amines behave as bases, readily accepting protons to form salts. Ethylamine is a stronger base than ammonia because the alkyl group has a positive inductive effect; phenylamine is a weaker base than ammonia because the phenyl group has a negative inductive effect.

■ Phenylamine reacts with nitrous acid on warming to give nitrogen and phenol. Below 5 °C, the products are phenyldiazonium chloride and water; this reaction is called diazotisation.

■ Diazonium salts react with other aromatic compounds to form dyes; this is known as a coupling reaction. Diazonium dyes are commercially useful. Some indicators are diazonium dyes. The colour of diazonium dyes arises from the extensively delocalised π-electron system (called a chromophore).

■ Phenylamine decolourises bromine water to form a white precipitate of 2,4,6-tribromophenylamine.

■ Amides are formed by the reaction of amines with acyl chlorides or with acid anhydrides. Amides are hydrolysed to form ammonia and carboxylic acids.

■ There are twenty-seven naturally occurring amino acids with the general formula $H_2NCHRCOOH$. 'R' may be H, CH_3 or another organic group. The amino group interacts with the acid group to form an internal salt or zwitterion. Amino acids react with both acids and bases to form salts.

■ With the exception of glycine, amino acids possess a chiral carbon atom (a chiral atom has four different groups attached) and so optical isomers are possible.

Questions

1 In aqueous solution, aminoethanoic acid (glycine, NH_2CH_2COOH) exists in different forms at different pH values. The zwitterionic form of aminoethanoic acid predominates between pH values of 2.35 and 9.78.

  a Draw displayed (full structural) formulae of the different forms of aminoethanoic acid at pH values (i) below 2.35, (ii) between 2.35 and 9.78 and (iii) above 9.78.

  b Aminoethanoic acid ($M_r = 75$) is a solid at room temperature, whereas 1-amino-butane ($M_r = 73$) is a liquid of low boiling point. With the aid of a diagram, explain this difference.

  c Two chiral forms are possible for 2-aminopropanoic acid (alanine, CH_3CHNH_2COOH). Draw diagrams to show the relationship between these two forms.

2 a Outline how you would prepare (i) ethylamine from bromoethane and (ii) phenylamine from nitrobenzene. Give all essential reagents and conditions for these conversions.

  b Describe and explain the order of base strengths of ethylamine and phenylamine relative to ammonia.

Polymerisation

1 describe the characteristics of addition polymerisation, as exemplified by poly(ethene) and poly(chloroethene);

2 show awareness of the difficulties involved in the disposal of poly(alkene)s;

3 describe the characteristics of condensation polymerisation, which is used to form polyesters and polyamides;

4 descibe the hydrolysis of proteins;

5 suggest the type of polymerisation reaction undergone by a given monomer or pair of monomers;

6 deduce the repeat unit of a polymer obtained from a given monomer or pair of monomers;

7 suggest the type of polymerisation reaction which produces a given section of a polymer molecule;

8 identify the monomer(s) present in a given section of a polymer molecule.

Polymers are macromolecules that are built up from very large numbers of small molecules known as monomers. Many natural polymers are known. For example, proteins are polymers of amino acids, natural rubber is a polymer of isoprene (page 25) and DNA is a polymer of nucleotides. Nucleotides consist of an organic base, such as adenine in adenosine triphosphate (ATP, the chemical that carries energy within cells), bonded to a sugar, such as ribose, which is in turn joined to one or more phosphate ions:

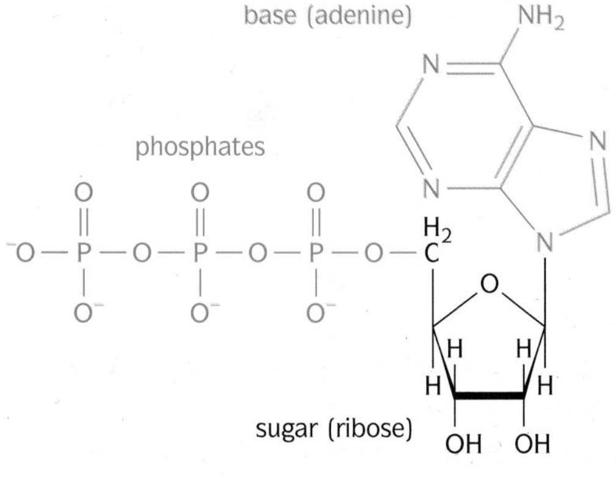

The polymer chain in DNA consists of a sugar–phosphate backbone. Two such backbones are linked by hydrogen bonds between pairs of bases to form a double helix (page 75).

Many polymers have been discovered by chemists in the twentieth century. Some of these polymers were made by modifying naturally occurring materials. For example, cellulose is converted into cellulose ethanoate (acetate) by an acylation reaction using ethanoyl chloride (page 68):

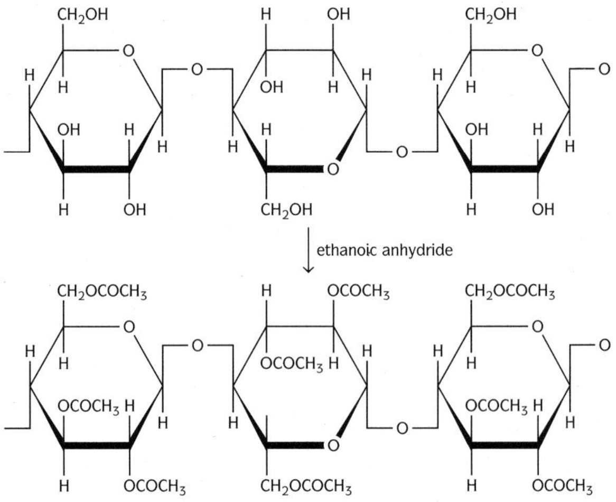

Other polymers were discovered by accident when the chemists concerned were pursuing a very different goal: examples include Bakelite® *(Box 8A)*, poly(tetrafluoroethene) and poly(ethene).

Nowadays, our understanding of the reactions and structures of polymers is much greater. Computer molecular modelling (chapter 9) is being used to design polymers with specific properties before the compounds are synthesised by chemists.

Polymer properties are dependent on a variety of factors such as chain length, crystallinity (crystallinity is greater when the molecules pack more closely), the degree of chain-branching or cross-linking and the strength of the intermolecular forces. The properties can be modified by the way the polymer is treated. For example, if the polymer is drawn (pulled through a small hole) whilst being formed into a fibre, the molecules tend to become more ordered. The intermolecular forces are

Box 8A Bakelite®

In 1872, Adolf von Baeyer made a resin by heating phenol with an aldehyde. He threw this resin away because he could not see a use for the material. The resin was re-investigated by Leo Hendrik Baekeland who, in 1910, set up a company to manufacture the material (which he called Bakelite®) for use in making electrical sockets and plugs. Since Baekeland's day, the material used in these components has changed several times. In the 1990s, polyester, polycarbonate and acrylonitrilebutadiene styrene copolymer (ABS) are used for these components *(figure 8.1)*. Once Bakelite® has been formed it cannot be melted, so it is a **thermosetting** polymer; the new materials can be melted and moulded many times (they are **thermoplastic** polymers), making fabrication much easier.

● *Figure 8.1* Electrical sockets and plugs are made from thermoplastic polymers.

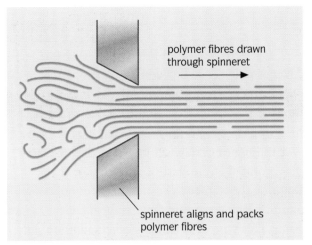

polymer fibres drawn through spinneret

spinneret aligns and packs polymer fibres

● *Figure 8.2* The packing of polymer chains increases the tensile strength of a fibre.

a

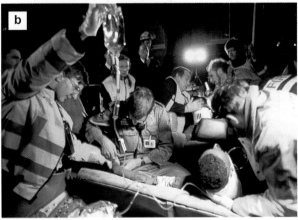

b

● *Figure 8.3*

a Canoes are often made from glass-reinforced poly(phenylethene).

b Blood bags are made from poly(chloroethene).

increased because the polymer chains are more closely packed; the tensile strength of the fibre is therefore greater *(figure 8.2)*. Properties are also modified by mixing the polymer with other materials. Glass fibre will produce a much stronger and more rigid material; plasticisers will produce a more flexible material. Canoes are made of glass-fibre-reinforced poly(phenylethene) *(figure 8.3a)*. The bags and tubing for blood transfusions are made from a poly(chloroethene) composite containing a plasticiser *(figure 8.3b)*.

The formation of polymers

Addition polymerisation

Alkenes polymerise by addition reactions. The alkene undergoes an addition to itself. As further molecules are added, a long molecular chain is built up. The reactions are initiated in various ways and an initiating chemical (**initiator**) may become incorporated at the start of the polymer chain. Ignoring the initiator, the empirical formula of an addition polymer is the same as the alkene it comes from. This type of reaction is called **addition poly- merisation**. Many useful polymers are obtained via addition polymerisation of different alkenes.

Poly(ethene) was first produced accidentally by Eric Fawcett and Reginald Gibson in 1933. The reaction involves ethene adding to itself in a chain reaction. It is a very rapid reaction, with chains of up to 10 000 ethene units being formed in one second. The product is a high-molecular-mass, straight-chain alkane. It is a polymer and is a member of a large group of materials generally known as **plastics**. The alkene from which it is made is called the **monomer**, and the section of polymer that the monomer forms is called the **repeat unit** (often shown within brackets in struc- tural formulae):

$$n \; \underset{H}{\overset{H}{\diagdown}} C = C \underset{H}{\overset{H}{\diagup}} \longrightarrow \left[\underset{H}{\overset{H}{\underset{|}{\overset{|}{C}}}} - \underset{H}{\overset{H}{\underset{|}{\overset{|}{C}}}} \right]_n$$

Skeletal formulae for two other important poly(alkene)s, poly(chloroethene) and poly(phenylethene), are:

poly(chloroethene)

poly(phenylethene)

They are more commonly known as PVC and polystyrene respectively. Note how the systematic name is derived by putting the systematic name of the monomer in brackets and prefixing this with 'poly'. The skeletal formulae of the monomers, chloroethene (traditionally vinyl chloride) and phenylethene (styrene), are as follows:

chloroethene   phenylethene

SAQ 8.1

a Acrylic fibre is often used in furnishing fabric or as a wool substitute in sweaters. It is an addition polymer of propenenitrile, $CH_2=CHCN$ (also called acrylonitrile). Write a balanced equation for the polymerisation of propenenitrile. Use a displayed formula in your equation to indicate the repeat unit of this polymer.

b A polymer which is often used to make plastic boxes for food storage has the structure:

$$CH_3 \quad CH_3 \quad CH_3 \quad CH_3$$

Draw displayed formulae to show (i) the repeat unit of this polymer and (ii) the monomer from which it is made. Label your diagrams with the appropriate systematic names.

There are several ways of bringing about the addition polymerisation of alkenes. These different methods produce polymers with different properties, which provide the wide variety of poly(alkene)s for the many applications of these versatile materials. Poly(alkene)s are thermoplastic, so they are easily made into different products by a variety of techniques. The molten polymer may be forced under pressure into a mould (**injection moulding**) or forced through a die to form pipes or other continuously moulded shapes (**extrusion moulding**). Fibres are produced by forcing the molten polymer through a die with fine holes (a spinneret). The emerging polymer is cooled in an air current to produce a continuous filament which

● *Figure 8.4* A stage in the production of poly(ethene) film.

may be spun into a yarn (the process is called **melt spinning**). Alternatively, a softened polymer sheet can be moulded into a shape under reduced pressure (**vacuum forming**) or under increased air pressure (**blow moulding**). An example of one of these techniques is shown in *figure 8.4*.

The use of poly(alkene)s has created a major problem when we wish to dispose of them. Sights like that shown in *figure 8.5* are only too familiar. As they are alkanes, they break down very slowly in the environment. They are resistant to most chemicals and to bacteria (they are non-biodegradable). It would be sensible to collect waste poly(alkene)s, sort them and recycle them into new products (*figure 8.6*). However, the current costs of recycling (in terms of the energy used in collecting and reprocessing the material) are often greater than those required for making new material. One alternative is to burn the poly(alkene)s to provide energy. They are potentially good fuels as they are

● *Figure 8.5* Polymer waste is not easy to dispose of – it is usually not biodegradable.

● *Figure 8.6* Recycling polymers is one way of combating the problem of polymer waste.

hydrocarbons, and they would reduce the amount of oil or other fossil fuels burned. They could be burnt with other combustible household waste, saving considerable landfill costs and providing a substantial alternative energy source. Modern technology is such that the waste could be burnt cleanly and with less pollution than from traditional, fossil-fuel power stations. The carbon dioxide produced would not add to the total emissions of this 'greenhouse gas' but would replace emissions from burning fossil fuels. Other pollutant gases, such as hydrogen chloride (produced by burning poly(chloroethene)), can be removed by the use of gas scrubbers. In a gas scrubber, acidic gases are dissolved and neutralised in a spray of alkali. New European Union legislation will require household waste incinerators to use them. A second option is to subject the polymers to high-temperature pyrolysis. This enables the polymers to be broken down into smaller, useful molecules. This is a process similar to the cracking of alkanes (page 21).

SAQ 8.2

Suggest some small molecules that might be produced by pyrolysis of poly(ethene). Explain how your suggestions would be useful.

Condensation polymerisation

Polyester formation

A significant proportion of clothing is made using polyester fibre. Polyester is also used to make plastic bottles for drinks (*figure 8.7*). Polyester is made by polymerising ethane-1,2-diol with

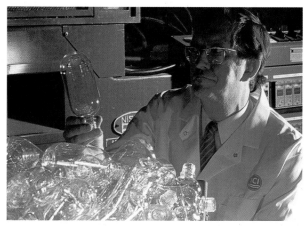

● **Figure 8.7** Poly(ethylene terephthalate), a polyester, is widely used for drinks bottles as a replacement for glass.

benzene-1,4-dicarboxylic acid (terephthalic acid). As each ester link is made, a water molecule is lost – a condensation reaction occurs. So the formation of a polyester is an example of **condensation polymerisation**. The reaction requires a catalyst such as antimony(III) oxide at about 280 °C. An equation for the reaction is:

The resulting polymer is fairly rigid because of the 1,4 links across the benzene ring. The 1,4 links produce a more linear polymer, which enables the polymer chains to pack more closely. Close-packing produces strong intermolecular forces, which enable the polymer to be spun into strong threads for the clothing industry.

SAQ 8.3

The external mirror housings of some vehicles have been made from PBT, or poly(butylene terephthalate). This material provides excellent protection to the mirror glass whilst driving off-road. The structure of PBT is:

Draw displayed formulae to show the two monomers used to make PBT. Write an equation for the reaction.

Polyamide formation

Wallace Carothers carried out research for Du Pont in 1928 in order to find new polymers that might be used for making fabric. At that time, it was known that wool and silk were proteins and that they contained the peptide linkage, –NHCO–. Because of this, Carothers set out to make polymers systematically, using condensation reactions involving amines and carboxylic acids.

In order to make a polymer, he realised that he needed monomers which had two functional groups present. The monomer could have an amino group at one end and a carboxylic acid group at the other. Alternatively, two monomer units could be used, one with an amino group at both ends, the other with a carboxylic acid group at both ends. Both approaches led to the discovery of new polymers, which are now widely used to make fibres.

Use of the diamine, 1,6-diaminohexane, together with the dicarboxylic acid, hexanedioic acid (commonly called adipic acid) produces a nylon called nylon-6,6. An amino group undergoes a condensation reaction with a carboxylic acid group. A water molecule is released and a C–N bond is formed. This can occur at each end of the two monomer molecules, so a condensation polymerisation is possible:

The product is a long chain of alternating monomer residues linked by amide groups, –NHCO–. Such polymers are called **polyamides**. Notice that each of the two monomer units contains six carbon atoms. This is why it is called nylon-6,6. Nylons are given names that indicate the number of carbon atoms in each monomer unit.

Nylon-6 is made from a single monomer containing six carbon atoms. This monomer is caprolactam, a cyclic amide. The caprolactam ring is polymerised to nylon-6 by heating:

Caprolactam is formed from 6-aminohexanoic acid by a condensation reaction:

● *Figure 8.8* Alex climbing Quietus on Stanage Edge, UK. He is using nylon rope and slings for protection. Nylon has a very high tensile strength, coupled with considerable elasticity. Climbers rely on these properties to minimise the effects of a fall.

Nylon forms a very strong fibre by melt spinning, during which the molecules become oriented along the axis of the fibre. This increases the opportunities for hydrogen bonds to form between the molecules. The hydrogen bonds also provide nylon with greater elasticity than is present in fibres without hydrogen bonds (such as poly(propene)). The hydrogen bonds tend to pull the molecules back to their original positions after the fibre has been stretched. This is why nylon is the most popular fibre for making tights. Tights made from many other fibres would tend to sag and lose their shape. The combination of strength and elasticity are also important properties in a climbing rope (*figure 8.8*).

Proteins and polypeptides

Proteins and polypeptides are important molecules in living organisms. Muscle and hair are composed of fibres containing long protein molecules. Enzymes are soluble proteins that catalyse many biochemical reactions. Proteins, like nylon, are also examples of polyamides.

Polypeptides are formed when amino acids undergo condensation polymerisation. Two amino acids join together via a peptide link to form a dipeptide and a water molecule – the peptide link

SAQ 8.4

Kevlar is a polyamide made by Du Pont. It has some remarkable properties, including fire resistance and a much higher tensile strength than steel. Kevlar is being used to make protective clothing for fire-fighters, bullet-proof vests, crash helmets for motor cyclists and tail fins for jumbo jets, and it is used instead of steel in radial tyres. The structure of this remarkable polymer is:

Draw a displayed formula to show the repeat unit in Kevlar and label the amide link clearly. Draw displayed formulae of the two monomer units required to make Kevlar. Write a balanced equation for the reaction.

is simply the name we use for the amide link in polypeptides and proteins:

$$H_2N-\underset{\underset{R}{|}}{\overset{\overset{H}{|}}{C}}-\overset{\overset{O}{\|}}{C}-OH \quad H-\underset{\underset{R}{|}}{\overset{\overset{H}{|}}{N}}-\underset{}{\overset{\overset{H}{|}}{C}}-COOH$$

peptide link ↘ H_2O ↗ atoms lost to form water
+

$$H_2N-\underset{\underset{R}{|}}{\overset{\overset{H}{|}}{C}}-\overset{\overset{O}{\|}}{C}-\underset{}{\overset{\overset{H}{|}}{N}}-\underset{\underset{R}{|}}{\overset{\overset{H}{|}}{C}}-COOH$$

Three amino acids produce a tripeptide and two water molecules. Polypeptides and proteins contain a large number of amino acid units. (Proteins generally have much larger relative molecular masses then polypeptides). In nature, proteins often consist of two or more polypeptides held together by intermolecular forces (such as hydrogen bonds). The sequence of amino acids in a protein is known as the **primary structure** of that protein.

Hydrolysis of a protein involves breaking the peptide links by reaction with water. So hydrolysis is the reverse of the condensation polymerisation of amino acids to form a protein. In living organisms, condensation polymerisation of amino acids and hydrolysis of proteins are both catalysed by enzymes. In the laboratory, acids or alkalis are used to catalyse the hydrolysis of proteins. Since each peptide link is broken, this is simply an extended example of the hydrolysis of an amide (page 81). Polyamides and polyesters are also hydrolysed to their monomers by refluxing with an acid catalyst.

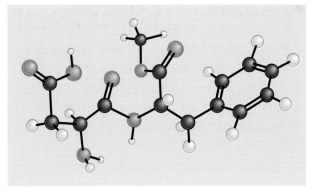

● *Figure 8.9* Aspartame.

SAQ 8.5

Aspartame is the methyl ester of the dipeptide formed between aspartic acid and phenylalanine *(figure 8.9)*. Its skeletal formula is:

It is used as a sweetener in many 'diet' soft drinks.

Aspartame has two links that may be hydrolysed.

a Copy the skeletal formula of aspartame. Mark the bonds that may be broken by hydrolysis, and label them with the names of the types of linkages present.

b Write a balanced equation for the acid hydrolysis of aspartame and name all the products.

SUMMARY

- Polymers are macromolecules that are built up from a very large number of small molecules known as monomers.

- Natural polymers include proteins, DNA and rubber. Many synthetic polymers have been discovered by accident (for example, poly(ethene) and Bakelite®). Polymers are now being designed to fulfil specific functions.

- The properties of polymers depend on chain length, inter-molecular forces, degree of chain branching, crystallinity and additives.

- Addition polymerisation occurs when a monomer joins to itself by an addition reaction. Alkenes polymerise in this way. Poly(ethene), poly(chloroethene) and poly(phenylethene) are important alkene polymers.

- Poly(alkene)s are non-biodegradable and are also very resistant to chemical decomposition. Disposal of poly(alkene) waste has become a problem. The waste may be buried or recycled and reprocessed. Alternatively, poly(alkene) waste may be incinerated as a 'clean' fuel. Gas scrubbers are required to remove polluting gases such as hydrogen chloride from poly(chloroethene) incineration.

- Condensation polymerisation involves the loss of a small molecule (usually water) in the reaction between two monomer molecules. Both polyesters and polyamides are formed by condensation polymerisation.

- Polyester is formed by condensation polymerisation of benzene-1,4-dicarboxylic acid with ethane-1,2-diol.

- Polyamides are formed by condensation polymerisation between an amine group and a carboxylic acid group. These groups may be at either end of the same monomer or on different monomers. Nylon-6,6 is formed in a condensation polymerisation between 1,6-diaminohexane and hexanedioic acid. Nylon-6 is formed by heating capro-lactam, which is produced from 6-aminohexanoic acid in a condensation reaction. The numbers in the names for nylons refer to the number of carbon atoms present in the monomers.

- Condensation polymerisation between the amino and carboxylic acid groups in amino acids produces a poly-peptide or protein. The amide links in these polymers are known as peptide links. Proteins and polypeptides are hydrolysed to amino acids, using enzymes or acids as catalysts.

Questions

1 The diagram below shows the structure of two repeat units of nylon-6,6. This form of nylon is made by the reaction of 1,6-diaminohexane with hexanedioic acid.

a Give **one** way in which the structure of this synthetic polymer is
  (i) similar to the structure of a protein,
  (ii) different from the structure of a protein.

b (i) Draw the displayed formula of 1,6-diaminohexane.
  (ii) Deduce the displayed formula of hexanedioic acid.

c With the aid of a diagram, show how a hydrogen bond may be formed between two peptide groups.

2 a Explain what is meant by the term *addition polymerisation*. Illustrate your answer with reference to a suitable example.

b Why has the disposal of poly(alkene) waste become a problem? Describe how this problem might be overcome.

c One class of important polymers are synthetic polyester fibres, such as Terylene®.
  (i) Give an equation for the formation of Terylene® from $HOCH_2CH_2OH$ and $HO_2CC_6H_4CO_2H$.
  (ii) Explain why Terylene® is a polyester.
  (iii) Draw a diagram to show two repeat units of Terylene®.

d (i) Aminoethanoic acid (glycine) and 2-aminopropanoic acid (alanine) can form two different dipeptides. Draw diagrams to show the structures of these two dipeptides. Explain what is meant by a *dipeptide*.
  (ii) Explain what is meant by *protein hydrolysis*, illustrating your answer by using one of the dipeptides you have drawn for part (i).

Designer molecules

1 summarise the reactions of the different functional groups that you met in chapters 1 to 8 of this book;

2 apply your knowledge and understanding to suggest synthetic routes of up to three steps, using familiar and unfamiliar reactions (given sufficient information);

3 understand how to characterise a product using analytical information from a variety of chemical and physical techniques;

4 explain the work of chemists in designing new molecules for different purposes.

How do we design molecules?

If we wish to design a molecule for a particular purpose, one approach is to identify the structural features that will achieve the desired result. The structural features of interest may be associated with the shape of the molecule or with the functional groups present. It is often possible to see a relationship between these structural features and the behaviour of the molecule in the body (**pharmacological activity**).

Some of the milder pain killers such as aspirin are derived from 2-hydroxybenzoic acid (salicylic

● **Figure 9.1** The leaves and bark of willow trees were used as a 'folk' medicine to reduce a fever and to relieve pain.

acid). (These compounds are also used to reduce the effects of fevers.) Many modern medicines are related to naturally occurring compounds used in 'folk' medicine. For example, a derivative of salicylic acid, called salicin, is present in willow bark and willow leaves *(figure 9.1)*. An infusion of willow leaves was recommended by Hippocrates (in 400 BC) for relieving pain whilst giving birth. A brew made from willow bark was used in the eighteenth century to reduce fever.

SAQ 9.1

The structures of aspirin, 2-hydroxybenzoic acid and salicin are:

aspirin	2-hydroxybenzoic acid (salicylic acid)	salicin

Copy these diagrams and circle the common structural feature.

The part of the molecules that you have circled in *SAQ 9.1* is the part which gives rise to their similar pharmacological activity. Such a structural feature is known as a **pharmacophore**. Investigation of other potential pain killers might focus on making similar molecules with this common structural feature.

SAQ 9.2

Which of the following compounds might have potential as mild pain killers?

A   B   C

Medicines act by binding to **receptor molecules** present in the body. In order to bind to a receptor molecule and produce the desired pharmacological effect, the medicine molecule must have the following features.

■ A shape which fits the receptor molecule.
■ Groups which are capable of forming intermolecular bonds to complementary groups on the receptor molecules. These intermolecular bonds may involve hydrogen bonding, ionic attraction, dipole–dipole forces or instantaneous dipole-induced dipole forces.

SAQ 9.3

Which of the following compounds would you choose to investigate for pharmacological activity at the receptor site shown in *figure 9.2*?

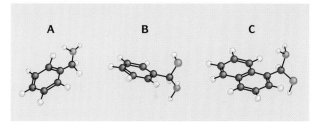

Computers are now used to examine the relationship between a molecule and a receptor site. Such **molecular modelling** has greatly speeded up the process of designing new medicines; the interactions and fit of a potential medicine with a biological receptor molecule can be studied before the

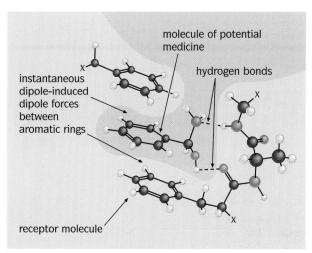

● **Figure 9.2** The interaction between a receptor molecule and a potential medicine.

medicine is synthesised *(figure 9.2)*. Before molecular modelling became available, the synthesis of a new medicine involved far more trial and error with many more compounds being prepared for testing. With molecular modelling, only those molecules that show potential after computer tests are made and tested. Molecular modelling on a computer thus provides a powerful tool for the design of medicines and many other compounds (such as pesticides or polymers).

Routes to new molecules

Even simple molecules such as aspirin may have several functional groups present. There may be a suitable, readily available molecule with a structure very close to the one desired. If such a starting material exists, it may be possible to achieve the desired product in a **one-step synthesis**. A one-step synthesis involves converting the starting material to the product by means of a single reaction. For example, a natural penicillin may be modified to produce a new penicillin with enhanced antibacterial activity. However, it is much more likely that several separate reactions may be needed to convert a suitable starting compound to the desired product: a **multi-step synthesis** is required.

Planning a multi-step synthesis requires a sound knowledge of many different reactions. The reactions that you have met in chapters 2 to 8 of this book provide you with the basis for planning the syntheses of a surprisingly wide range of organic compounds. We shall now review these reactions. This review should enable you to use reactions effectively in planning multi-step syntheses of your own, as well as helping you to learn the reactions more thoroughly. The reactions are best divided into two groups: aliphatic reactions and aromatic reactions.

Aliphatic reactions

You may have already seen a connection between the reactions of a number of functional groups. These are summarised in *figure 9.3*, which shows the names of the functional groups, together with arrows to indicate the interconversions possible.

Aromatic reactions

Figure 9.4 provides you with the framework for reactions involving aromatic compounds.

Try copying and displaying the reaction summaries (from *figures 9.3* and *9.4*) where you will look at them regularly – this will help you to learn the reactions and their conditions. Note the central role of halogenoalkanes in these synthetic

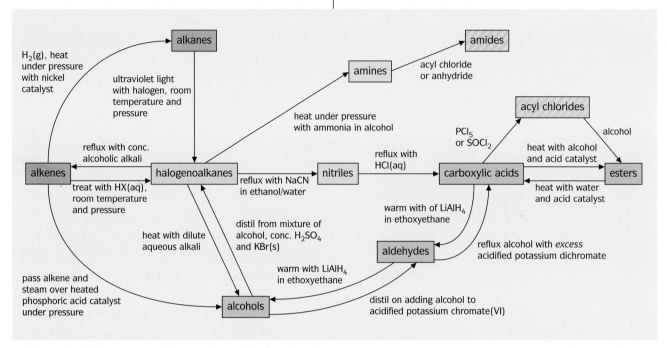

● **Figure 9.3** A summary of the reactions of the functional groups.

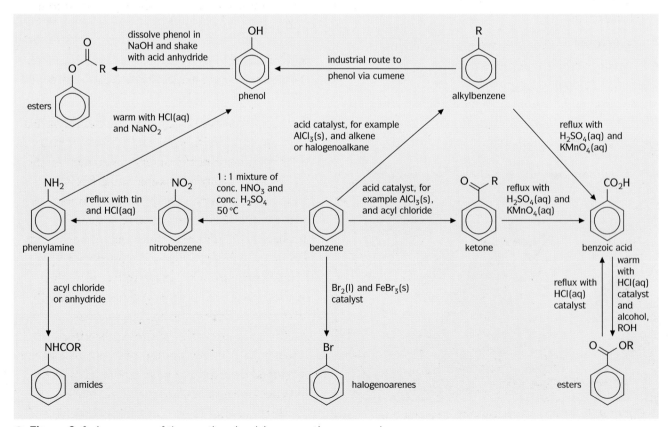

● **Figure 9.4** A summary of the reactions involving aromatic compounds.

routes (this was referred to in chapter 3). The frameworks given in *figures 9.3* and *9.4* are also suitable for making annotated charts to provide summaries of reaction mechanisms or for summaries of tests for the different groups.

You can use the reaction summaries to plan multi-step syntheses. Suppose we wish to convert ethene to ethanoic acid. A possible route is to convert ethene to ethanol, which is then oxidised to ethanoic acid. Alternatively, ethene could be converted to bromoethane, which is then hydrolysed to ethanol, and this is oxidised to ethanoic acid. This alternative involves an extra reaction step; you should usually try to complete a synthesis in as few steps as possible (remember that material is lost at each stage when preparing organic compounds: reaction yields seldom approach 100%).

SAQ 9.4

Outline how you might carry out the following conversions involving two- or three-step syntheses. Include the conditions required for the reactions. Start by drawing the structural formulae of the initial and final compounds.

a Ethene to ethylamine.

b Benzaldehyde to ethyl benzoate.

c 1-Bromopropane to butanoic acid.

d Butan-2-one to 2-aminobutane.

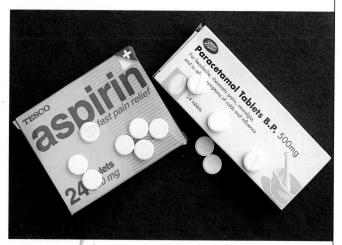

● **Figure 9.5** Aspirin and paracetamol are products of multi-step syntheses.

Carrying out a synthesis

The synthesis of a simple medicine, such as paracetamol or aspirin *(figure 9.5)*, can provide an exciting basis for a project. The structures of paracetamol and aspirin are:

aspirin   paracetamol

When considering such a project, there are a number of criteria to consider. A good project will have sufficient scope to allow you to demonstrate your skills in planning, implementing, interpreting and concluding as well as researching. As these skills all carry equal weight in the assessment of your project, it is important that you design your project in such a way as to allow you to address each skill.

SAQ 9.5

Outline a possible route from phenol to paracetamol.

If you have answered *SAQ 9.5*, you should have a three-step synthesis. At the end of the first step you will have a mixture of isomers to separate. As they are solids, this may be possible using fractional crystallisation. Alternatively, chromatography may be used. The second step involves a steam distillation. All this takes time, and in the limited amount of practical time that you have for your project you may only manage to complete this synthesis two (possibly three) times. As this will produce very limited results, you will have insufficient opportunity to discuss the effects of variables (a planning subskill) or to produce a well-developed discussion of your results (interpreting and concluding skills). You may have made a couple of samples of paracetamol with yields and melting points to comment on, but little else.

A better approach for the purpose of a project is to concentrate on investigating the best conditions to optimise the yield at a particular step. Studying the effect of different conditions on a single reaction step will give a range of results for discussion. For example, the first step to paracetamol involves the nitration of phenol. Different conditions could be tried – a range of temperatures; a range of concentrations of nitric acid; different lengths of reaction time; and so on. Analysis of the products obtained in this first step may be carried out at intervals during the reaction using thin-layer chromatography. Comparisons may be made of product yield and purity. If you carry out an investigation in this way, you will be working in the same way as a process development chemist, repeating the reaction whilst making minor changes to achieve the optimum yield (you could even consider costs of energy and materials). You will have extensive results to discuss and you can still make a sample of paracetamol.

SAQ 9.6

Outline a possible conversion of phenol to aspirin via 2-hydroxybenzoic acid. Suggest a possible sequence of experiments to investigate optimising the yield of aspirin. Indicate which variables are being studied and which are being controlled.

Deciding on masses of reactants

If you choose to carry out an organic synthesis for your project, you will need to calculate the appropriate reacting masses (for liquids you may choose to use volumes, for solutions you will need to know the concentrations to decide on the volumes required). These will need to be appropriate for the capacity of the reaction flask that you will use.

Calculate reacting quantities using the stoichiometric equation for the reaction. The approach is similar to that used in chapter 1 (page 13) when deciding which reactant is in excess for the calculation of percentage yield. You may wish to use exact amounts or to have one (possibly cheaper) reagent in excess.

SAQ 9.7

Write a balanced equation for the conversion of 2-hydroxybenzoic acid to aspirin using ethanoic anhydride. Calculate the mass of ethanoic anhydride required to react with 2.0 g of 2-hydroxybenzoic acid.

In chapter 1 (page 14) we discussed the calculation of the yield of product after a single reaction step. To calculate the overall yield for a multi-step synthesis, you multiply the percentage yield of the last step by the fractional yield for the preceding steps. For example, if a three-step synthesis has yields of 70% at each step, the overall yield is:

$$\frac{70}{100} \times \frac{70}{100} \times 70\% = 34.3\%$$

Purifying and identifying the product

You will need to consider how to purify your product (called the **target molecule** in the pharmaceutical industry). Confirming that you have made the target molecule is called **characterisation**. This can be done in a variety of ways. Chromatography can be particularly useful for confirming purity as well as identity. Other methods of characterising a product include melting-point and boiling-point determinations, electrophoresis, mass spectrometry and the use of spectroscopic techniques. Most of these techniques are described in outline in chapter 1. You may have the opportunity to study them in depth in the *Methods of Analysis and Detection* module.

Safety

Before you start any practical work, you must check your proposed experiments for hazards and establish the precautions that you need to take to work safely. This is called a **risk assessment** and your teacher will provide guidance on how to do this. Your teacher will also expect to check your risk assessment before allowing you to start practical work.

Designing molecules in industry

The use of molecular modelling in the design of a new medicine has already been mentioned, as have the many tools used by chemists in the characterisation of a compound. The use of all these tools has given us greatly increased capabilities in our search for new medicines. However, the search would not be possible without a wide range of other specialists including botanists, instrument designers and operators, computer scientists, biochemists, statisticians, geneticists and molecular biologists. All these specialists work with chemists in a team with a common goal. Any one of them might have the idea which provides the breakthrough to a new medicine. In terms of a career, working in such a team must be one of the most creative activities possible. Indeed, Lord Porter (winner of the 1967 Nobel prize for chemistry) has said: 'We chemists have not yet discovered how to make gold but, in contentment and satisfaction with our lot, we are the richest people on Earth.'

SUMMARY

■ Molecular design of a new medicine is made possible with a sound understanding of the structural features that produce medical effects. The computerised study of the interactions between molecules and biological receptors has become a powerful tool in the search for new medicines.

■ Many multi-step syntheses can be planned using the reactions of the functional groups discussed in this book.

■ The preparation of a new compound will involve safety considerations, making decisions on quantities of reagents to use, establishing that conditions provide the best yield and purification and characterisation of the product.

■ In the design and production of a new medicine, chemists work as part of a team that includes a wide range of other specialists such as molecular biologists, chemical engineers and computer scientists.

Questions

1 a Complete the reaction scheme below which starts with the compound ethene. Draw the structural formulae of the principal organic products or intermediate compounds **A** to **F**.

b Identify the reagents **X** and **Y**.

2 Outline the reactions you would use to complete each of the syntheses shown below in not more than three steps. For each reaction, state the reagents you would use and the conditions under which the reaction could occur. (You are not expected to describe how any of the products are purified.)

3 Make a copy of *figure 9.3*. Use it to make summaries of the tests that you have met in chapters 2 to 8. Record on your chart, next to each type of compound, the test reagent(s) and what you would see. For example, next to alkenes you could write 'orange bromine water is decolourised when it is shaken with the compound.'

Answers to self-assessment questions

Chapter 1

1.1 See *figure*.

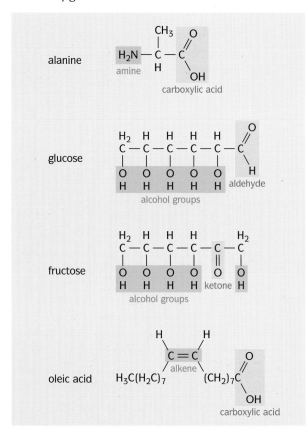

● **Answer for** SAQ 1.1

1.2 See *figure*.

● **Answer for** SAQ 1.2

1.3 As 12 g of carbon are present in 1 mol (= 44 g) CO_2,

$$\text{mass of carbon in } 0.4800\text{ g of } CO_2 = \frac{12}{44} \times 0.4800\text{ g}$$
$$= 0.1309\text{ g}$$
$$= \text{mass of carbon in } \mathbf{W}$$

As 2 g of hydrogen are present in 1 mol (= 18 g) H_2O,

$$\text{mass of hydrogen in } 0.1636\text{ g of } H_2O = \frac{2}{18} \times 0.1636\text{ g}$$
$$= 0.0182\text{ g}$$
$$= \text{mass of hydrogen in } \mathbf{W}$$

As 14 g of nitrogen are present in 1 mol (= 17 g) NH_3,

$$\text{mass of nitrogen in } 0.0618\text{ g of } NH_3 = \frac{14}{17} \times 0.0618\text{ g}$$
$$= 0.0509\text{ g}$$
$$= \text{mass of nitrogen in } \mathbf{W}$$

Hence

$$\text{mass of C, H and N in } 0.2000\text{ g of } \mathbf{W} = \begin{array}{l}(0.1309 + 0.0182 \\ \quad + 0.0509)\text{ g}\end{array}$$
$$= 0.2000\text{ g}$$

As this is the same as the total mass of the sample, $\mathbf{W}$ contains only C, H and N.

Now we calculate the numbers of moles of C, H and N:

	C	H	N
Mass/g	0.1309	0.0182	0.0509
Amount/ mol	0.1309/12 = 1.091×10^{-2}	0.0182/1 = 1.82×10^{-2}	0.0509/14 = 3.636×10^{-3}

Divide by the smallest amount to give whole numbers:

Atoms/ mol	3	5	1

Hence the empirical formula of $\mathbf{W}$ is C_3H_5N.

98

1.4 Molecular ion peak is at mass to charge ratio of 88. Empirical formula, C_2H_4O, has a relative molecular mass of 44. As the molecular ion mass is double this value, the molecular formula is $C_4H_8O_2$.

1.5

	Mass/charge ratio	Fragment ion
A	29	$CH_3CH_2^+$
B	43	CH_3CO^+
C	45	$CH_3CH_2O^+$

1.6

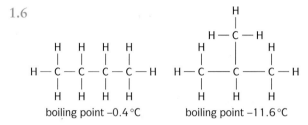

boiling point –0.4 °C   boiling point –11.6 °C

1.7 See *figure*.

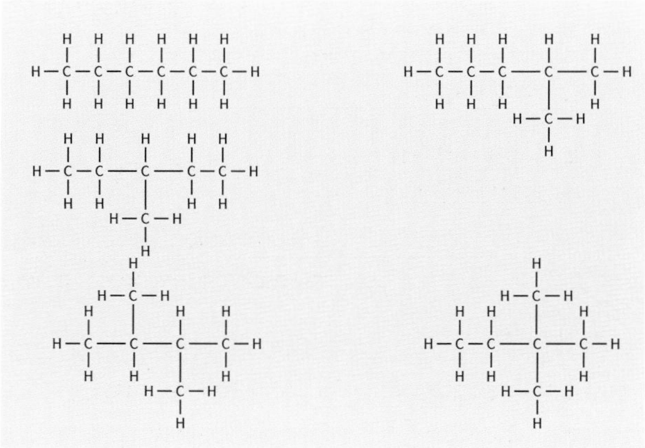

● ***Answer for*** SAQ 1.7

1.8 See *figure*.

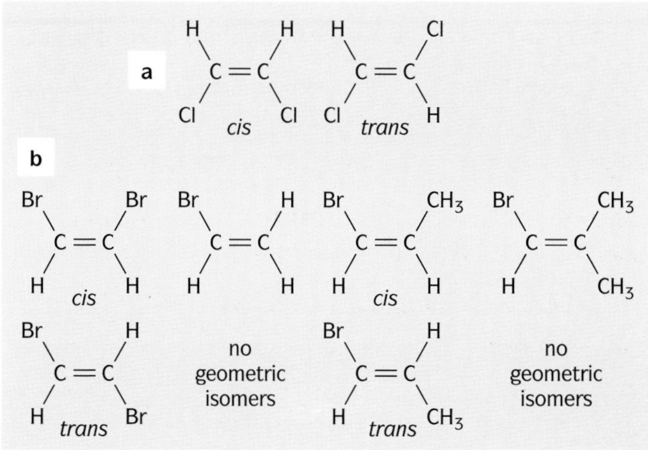

● ***Answer for*** SAQ 1.8

1.9 See *figure*.

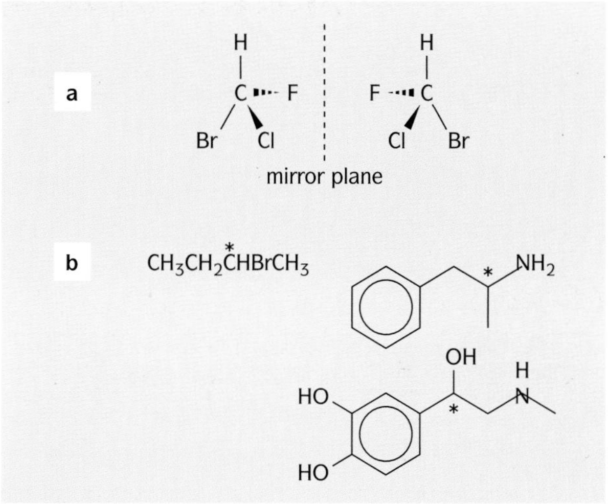

● ***Answer for*** SAQ 1.9

1.10 a **A** pentan-3-ol

 B pentan-2-one

 C 2-methylbutanoic acid

 D 2,2-dimethylpropanal

 E 4-chloronitrobenzene

 b See *figure*.

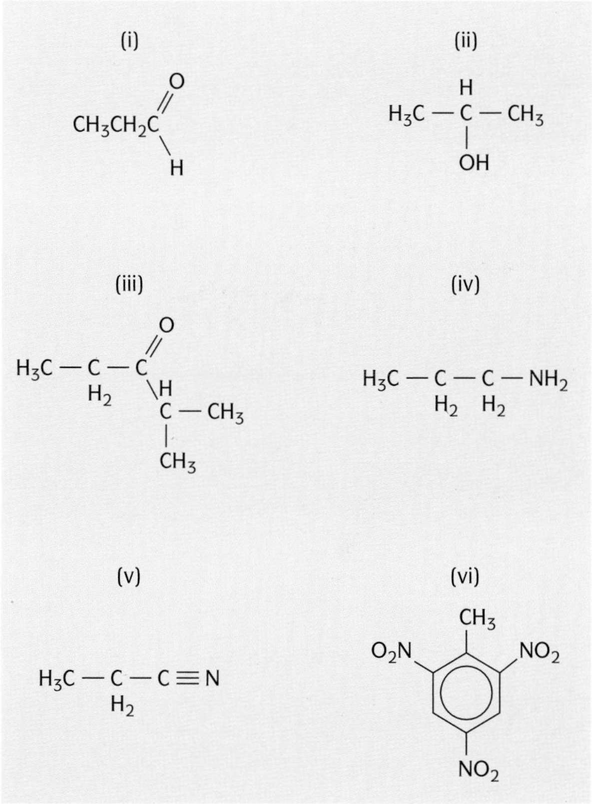

● ***Answer for*** SAQ 1.10b

1.11 1 mol of butan-1-ol will produce 1 mol of 1-bromobutane. The quantity of butan-1-ol will determine the yield as the other reagents are in excess.

1 mol of butan-1-ol, C_4H_9OH, has a relative molecular mass of
$4 \times 12 + 9 \times 1 + 1 \times 16 + 1 = 74\,g$

1 mol of 1-bromobutane, C_4H_9Br, has a relative molecular mass of
$4 \times 12 + 9 \times 1 + 80 = 137\,g$

Hence

$$\text{maximum yield of 1-bromobutane} = 10 \times \frac{137}{74} = 18.5\,g$$

$$\text{percentage yield} = \frac{12}{18.5} \times 100 = 65\%$$

1.12 See *figure*.

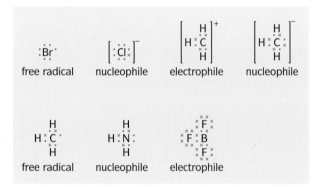

● **Answer for** SAQ 1.12

Free radicals have seven outer-shell electrons, electrophiles have six and nucleophiles have eight.

Chapter 2

2.1

Possible reactions include:

$CH_3CH_2CH_2CH_2CH_3 \longrightarrow CH_3CH_2CH_3 + H_2C = CH_2$

$\longrightarrow CH_3CH_2CH_2CH = CH_2 + H_2$

$\longrightarrow CH_3CH_2CH = CHCH_3 + H_2$

$\longrightarrow CH_3CH_3 + CH_3CH = CH_2$

$\longrightarrow CH_2 = CHCH = CHCH_3 + 2H_2$

$\longrightarrow H_3C - \overset{\overset{\displaystyle H}{|}}{C} - C = CH_2 + H_2$
$\qquad\qquad \underset{\displaystyle CH_3}{|} \quad \overset{\displaystyle H}{}$

2.2 a $C_4H_{10}(g) + 6.5O_2(g)$
$\longrightarrow 4CO_2(g) + 5H_2O(l)$

b Energy absorbed on breaking bonds in reactants

$= 3E(C–C) + 10E(C–H) + 6.5E(O=O)$

$= 3 \times 347 + 10 \times 413 + 6.5 \times 498$

$= +8408\,kJ\,mol^{-1}$

c Energy released on forming bonds in products

$= -8E(C=O) - 10E(O–H)$

$= -8 \times 805 - 10 \times 464$

$= -11080\,kJ\,mol^{-1}$

d $\Delta H_c = +8408 - 11080$
$= -2672\,kJ\,mol^{-1}$

e The reaction has a large activation energy due to the relatively high bond energies of C–C and C–H bonds.

2.3 a $Br_2(l)$ and $Cl_2(g)$ only – the others are in aqueous solution and are already ionised.

b $C_4H_{10}(g) + Br_2(l) \longrightarrow C_4H_9Br(l) + HBr(g)$

$C_4H_{10}(g) + Cl_2(g) \longrightarrow C_4H_9Cl(l) + HCl(g)$

2.4 See *figure*.

molecule is planar

● **Answer for** SAQ 2.4

2.5 a **D** and **E** can also exist as *cis–trans* isomers.

b

cis-pent-2-ene   *trans*-pent-2-ene

2.6 a

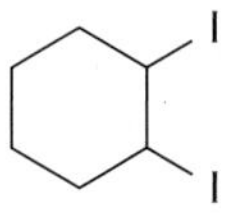

Shake with iodine dissolved in a non-polar solvent.

b

(structure: cyclohexane ring with H and I substituents)

Shake with concentrated hydroiodic acid.

c

(structure: cyclohexane ring with H and OH substituents)

Pass vapour with steam over a solid acid catalyst.

2.7 a

$$CH_3 - \overset{\overset{H}{|}}{C} = \overset{\overset{H}{|}}{C} - CH_3 + HBr \longrightarrow CH_3 - \overset{\overset{H}{|}}{\underset{\underset{H}{|}}{C}} - \overset{\overset{H}{|}}{\underset{\underset{Br}{|}}{C}} - CH_3$$

b

$$CH_3 - \overset{\overset{H}{|}}{\underset{\underset{OH}{|}}{C}} - \underset{\underset{OH}{|}}{CH_2}$$

2.8 a

$$\overset{H_3C}{\underset{H_3C}{>}}C = C\overset{CH_3}{\underset{H}{<}} + 3[O] \longrightarrow \overset{H_3C}{\underset{H_3C}{>}}C = O + O = C\overset{CH_3}{\underset{OH}{<}}$$

b

$$\overset{H_3C}{\underset{H_3C}{>}}C = C\overset{CH_3}{\underset{CH_3}{<}} + 2[O] \longrightarrow 2\, O = C\overset{CH_3}{\underset{CH_3}{<}}$$

2.9 See *figure*.

a

$$H \overset{\times}{\underset{\times}{:}} \overset{H}{\underset{}{C}} \overset{\times}{\underset{\times}{:}} \overset{H}{\underset{}{C}} \overset{\times}{\underset{\times}{:}} H$$
$$\overset{\times}{\underset{\times}{Br}} \oplus$$

The positive carbon atom has six electrons in its outer shell. It gains two more by accepting a lone-pair from the bromide ion.

b

$$\overset{H}{\underset{H}{>}}C = C\overset{H}{\underset{H}{<}} \longrightarrow H - \overset{\overset{H}{|}}{\underset{\underset{H}{|}}{C}} - \overset{\overset{H}{|}}{\underset{\underset{H}{|}}{C}}^{\oplus} - H \longrightarrow H - \overset{\overset{H}{|}}{\underset{\underset{H}{|}}{C}} - \overset{\overset{H}{|}}{\underset{\underset{Cl}{|}}{C}} - H$$

$H_{\delta+}$ Cl $^{\delta-}$ Cl: $^{\ominus}$

● **Answer for** SAQ 2.9

2.10 a The attacking species involved in the addition to benzene is a free radical.

b The attacking species involved in the addition of chlorine to an alkene is an electrophile.

2.11 See *figure*.

Likely products:

2,4-dinitromethylbenzene

(structure: benzene ring with CH₃, NO₂ and NO₂)

2,6-dinitromethylbenzene

(structure: benzene ring with CH₃, O₂N and NO₂)

Unlikely products:

2,3-dinitromethylbenzene

(structure: benzene ring with CH₃, NO₂ and NO₂)

3,4-dinitromethylbenzene

(structure: benzene ring with CH₃, NO₂ and NO₂)

3,5-dinitromethylbenzene

(structure: benzene ring with CH₃, O₂N and NO₂)

2,5-dinitromethylbenzene

(structure: benzene ring with CH₃, NO₂ and O₂N)

● **Answer for** SAQ 2.11

2.12 See *figure*.

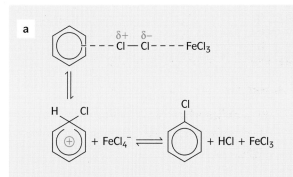

a

$$\delta+ \quad \delta-$$
benzene ---- Cl — Cl ---- FeCl₃

⇅

$$\overset{H \quad Cl}{\underset{\oplus}{benzene}} + FeCl_4^- \rightleftharpoons \overset{Cl}{benzene} + HCl + FeCl_3$$

b

(i) *(structure: benzene ring with CH₃ and Cl, ortho)*   *(structure: benzene ring with CH₃ and Cl, para)*

(ii) *(structure: benzene ring with CH₂Cl)*

● **Answer for** SAQ 2.12

2.13 a *(structure: benzene ring with CH₃ and CH₂CH₃, ortho)*   *(structure: benzene ring with CH₃ and CH₂CH₃, para)*

b

CH₃ — OSO₃H (on ring)   CH₃ ... OSO₃H (para on ring)

Chapter 3

3.1 $CH_3CH_2CH_2I$: 1-iodopropane;
$CH_3CHBrCH_3$: 2-bromopropane;
$CBrF_2CBrF_2$: 1,2-dibromo-1,1,2,2-tetrafluoroethane.

3.2 Structural isomerism.

$$H_3C - \overset{\overset{\displaystyle CH_3}{|}}{\underset{\underset{\displaystyle H}{|}}{C}} - CH_2Cl$$

This is a primary chloroalkane.

3.3 **a** 1-chloropropane is polar and has dipole–dipole intermolecular forces that are stronger then the instantaneous dipole-induced dipole forces in non-polar butane. More energy is needed to overcome the inter-molecular forces in 1-chlorobutane, so its boiling point is higher.

b 1-chloropropane attracts water molecules by dipole–dipole forces that are weaker than the hydrogen bonds in water. An input of energy would be required for 1-chloro-propane to mix with water and break some of these hydrogen bonds.

3.4

$$H_3C - \overset{\overset{\displaystyle CH_3}{|}}{\underset{\underset{\displaystyle CH_3}{|}}{C}} - Br + OH^- \longrightarrow H_3C - \overset{\overset{\displaystyle CH_3}{|}}{\underset{\underset{\displaystyle CH_3}{|}}{C}} - OH + Br^-$$

2-methylpropan-2-ol

3.5 Ammonia behaves as a nucleophile because the nitrogen atom possesses a lone-pair of electrons, which will form a covalent bond to carbon:

$$H_3C\text{—}\overset{\delta-}{C}\text{—}\overset{\delta+}{Br} \longrightarrow H_3C\text{—}\overset{\oplus}{C}\text{—}NH_3 + Br^- \longrightarrow H_3C\text{—}C\text{—}NH_2 + HBr$$

(with NH_3 attacking)

The hydrogen bromide will be neutralised by excess ammonia to form ammonium bromide:

$$HBr + NH_3 \longrightarrow NH_4Br$$

3.6 **a**

$$\left[:C \overset{\times}{\underset{\times}{\cdot}} N \overset{\times}{\underset{\times}{\times}} \right]^-$$

b

$$H_3C\text{—}\overset{\delta-}{\underset{\delta+}{C}}\text{—}Br \longrightarrow H_3C\text{—}C\text{—}CN + Br^-$$

(with $:CN^-$ attacking)

c The nitrogen atom may donate its lone-pair of electrons to the carbon atom on the bromoethane. However, carbon forms a stronger bond to carbon than to nitrogen. (Bond energies: $E(C\text{–}C) = 347\,kJ\,mol^{-1}$, $E(C\text{–}N) = 286\,kJ\,mol^{-1}$.)

Chapter 4

4.1 Energy is absorbed when a bond is broken.

In order from strongest to weakest:
$E(O\text{–}H) > E(C\text{–}H) > E(C\text{–}O) > E(C\text{–}C)$

4.2 **a** C–O.

b The oxygen atom is very electronegative compared to hydrogen or carbon.

c Both electrophiles and nucleophiles can form covalent bonds to carbon. An electrophile has a positively charged atom, which is attracted by an electron-rich centre. A nucleophile has a lone-pair of electrons, which is attracted to a positively charged centre.

4.3 See *figure*.

a and b $H \overset{\times}{\underset{\times}{:}} \overset{\times\times}{\underset{\times}{Br}}$ $\quad\overset{\delta+}{}\ \overset{\delta-}{}$

c $H\text{—}\overset{\overset{H}{|}}{\underset{\underset{H}{|}}{C}}\text{—}\overset{\overset{H}{|}}{\underset{\underset{H}{|}}{\overset{\delta+}{C}}}\text{—}\overset{\delta-}{O}\text{—}H$

d and e

$$H_3C\text{—}\overset{\overset{H}{|}}{\underset{\underset{H}{|}}{\overset{\delta+}{C}}}\text{—}\overset{\delta-}{O}\text{—}H \longrightarrow H_3C\text{—}\overset{\overset{H}{|}}{\underset{\underset{H}{|}}{C}}\text{—}Br + H^+ + {}^-OH$$

(with Br below)

$$\longrightarrow CH_3CH_2Br + H_2O$$

● *Answer for* SAQ 4.3

4.4 The hydrolysis of bromoethane requires aqueous ethanolic alkali and heat. The reverse reaction requires distillation with an excess of sodium bromide and concentrated sulphuric acid (no water is added). In the forward reaction, excess of water moves the reaction in the direction of hydrolysis. In the reverse reaction, absence of water and excess of hydrogen bromide (generated from the concentrated sulphuric acid and sodium bromide) moves the reaction towards the formation of bromoethane.

4.5 a

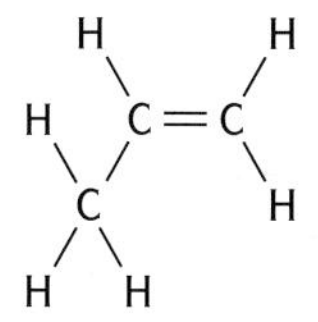

b $CH_3CH(OH)CH_3 \longrightarrow CH_3CH=CH_2 + H_2O$

4.6 a

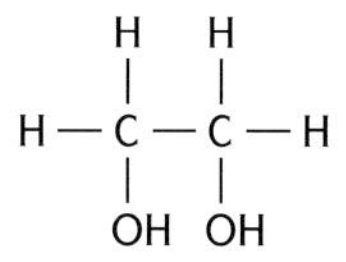

b It mixes freely with water because the intermolecular forces in both water and ethane-1,2-diol are hydrogen bonds – there will be little exchange of energy when they are mixed.

4.7 See *figure*.

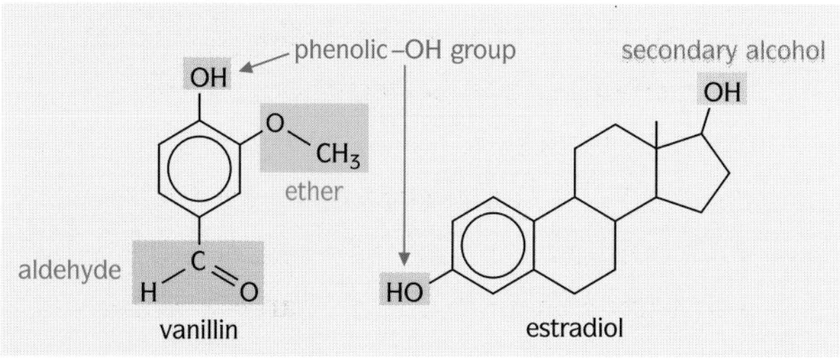

● **Answer for** SAQ 4.7

4.8 The bromine molecule is polarised by the delocalised π electrons on phenol. (The enhanced reactivity of the benzene ring, caused by the –OH group, is also required. Aqueous bromine will not react with benzene.)

4.9

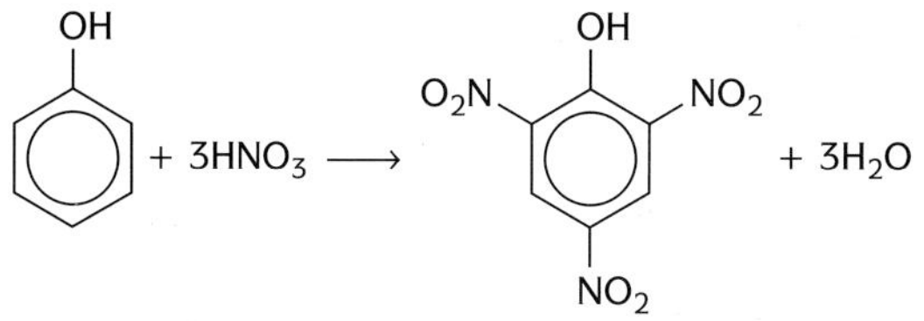

OH + 3HNO₃ ⟶ (2,4,6-trinitrophenol) + 3H₂O

Chapter 5

5.1 See *figure*.

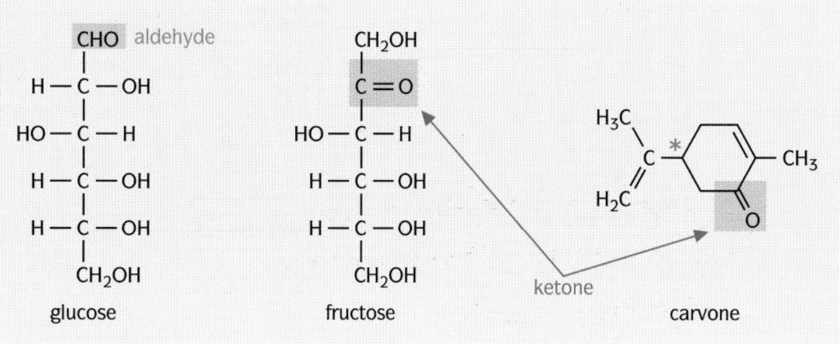

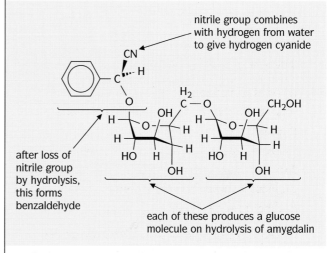

● **Answer for** SAQ 5.1

5.2 a See *figure*.

nitrile group combines with hydrogen from water to give hydrogen cyanide

after loss of nitrile group by hydrolysis, this forms benzaldehyde

each of these produces a glucose molecule on hydrolysis of amygdalin

● **Answer for** SAQ 5.2a

b Hydrolysis involves the breaking of a covalent bond by reaction with water.

5.3 The hydrocarbon part of the molecules is only attracted to other molecules by weak, instantaneous dipole-induced dipole forces. The carbonyl group has a permanent dipole and will hydrogen bond to water molecules. Aldehydes and ketones with less than four carbon atoms are miscible (they mix freely) with water because the intermolecular forces in the mixture are similar in strength to those in the separate liquids. As the length of the carbon chain is increased, the intermolecular forces in the organic compounds decrease and become too weak for the hydrogen bonding between water molecules to be disrupted.

5.4 a

$$H_3C - \underset{H_2}{C} - \underset{\underset{|}{H}}{\overset{\overset{OH}{|}}{C}} - CH_3$$

b

$$H_3C - \underset{H_2}{C} - \underset{H_2}{C} - CH_3$$

c

$$H_3C - \underset{H_2}{C} - \underset{H_2}{C} - CH_2OH$$

5.5

$$H - \underset{\underset{|}{H}}{\overset{\overset{H}{|}}{C}} - \underset{\underset{|}{H}}{\overset{\overset{H}{|}}{C}} - \underset{\underset{|}{H}}{\overset{\overset{H}{|}}{C}} - \overset{\overset{O}{\parallel}}{C}_{O - H}$$

5.6 a The following compounds give a pale yellow precipitate when warmed with alkaline aqueous iodine: (i) CH_3COCH_3; (iii) $CH_3CH(OH)CH_3$; (iv) CH_3CH_2OH.

b The products are: (i) CHI_3 and CH_3COO^-; (iii) CHI_3 and CH_3COO^-; (iv) CHI_3 and $HCOO^-$.

Chapter 6

6.1 a Ester.

b Carboxylic acid.

c Acyl chloride.

6.2 a $\diagup\!\!\diagup\!\!\diagup\!\!\diagup\!\!\diagup\!\!\diagup\!\!\diagup\!\!\diagup$COOH

b $\diagup\!\!\diagup\!\!\diagup\!\!\diagup\!\!\diagdown\!\!\diagup\!\!\diagup\!\!\diagup$COOH

c Octadeca-*cis*-9-*cis*-12-dienoic acid.

d

$$H - \underset{\underset{|}{H}}{\overset{\overset{H}{|}}{C}} - \underset{\underset{\underset{|}{H}}{\overset{\overset{|}{H-C-H}}{|}}}{\overset{}{C}} - \overset{\overset{O}{\parallel}}{C}_{O - H} \quad \text{2-methylpropanoic acid}$$

e

$$H - \underset{\underset{|}{H}}{\overset{\overset{H}{|}}{C}} - \underset{\underset{|}{H}}{\overset{\overset{H}{|}}{C}} - \overset{\overset{O}{\parallel}}{C}_{O - H} \quad \text{propanoic acid}$$

f 3-methylbutan-1-ol. It is a reduction.

$$H_3C - \underset{H}{\overset{\overset{CH_3}{|}}{C}} - \underset{H_2}{C} - COOH + 4[H] \longrightarrow H_3C - \underset{H}{\overset{\overset{CH_3}{|}}{C}} - \underset{H_2}{C} - CH_2OH + H_2O$$

6.3 In order of increasing acid strength:

$CH_2ICOOH < CH_2BrCOOH < CH_2ClCOOH < CH_2FCOOH$

6.4 a $Zn(s) + 2CH_3CH_2COOH(aq)$
$\longrightarrow (CH_3CH_2COO)_2Zn(aq) + H_2(g)$

b $Na_2CO_3(aq) + 2HCOOH(aq)$
$\longrightarrow 2HCOONa(aq) + CO_2(g) + H_2O(l)$

c $MgO(s) + 2CH_3COOH(aq)$
$\longrightarrow (CH_3COO)_2Mg(aq) + H_2O(l)$

d

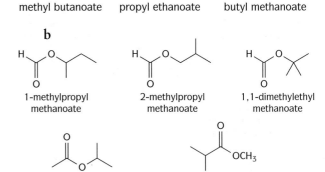

6.5 a $CH_3CH_2COOH(l) + CH_3OH(l)$
$\longrightarrow CH_3CH_2COOCH_3(l) + H_2O(l)$

b $CH_3CH_2COOH(l) + PCl_5(s)$
$\longrightarrow CH_3CH_2COCl(l) + HCl(g) + POCl_3(l)$

6.6 a $CH_3CH_2COCl(l) + H_2O(l)$
$\longrightarrow CH_3CH_2COOH(l) + HCl(g)$

b $CH_3CH_2COCl(l) + CH_3OH(l)$
$\longrightarrow CH_3CH_2COOCH_3(l) + HCl(g)$

c $CH_3CH_2COCl(l) + CH_3CH_2NH_2(aq)$
$\longrightarrow CH_3CH_2CONHCH_2CH_3(s) + HCl(g)$

6.7 a

methyl butanoate   propyl ethanoate   butyl methanoate

b

1-methylpropyl methanoate   2-methylpropyl methanoate   1,1-dimethylethyl methanoate

1-methylethyl ethanoate   methyl 2-methylpropanoate

Pentanoic acid, $CH_3CH_2CH_2CH_2COOH$, and structural isomers of this and other acids.

Methoxybutan-2-one, $CH_3OCH_2COCH_2CH_3$, and structural isomers of this with an ether plus a ketone or an aldehyde group.

Cyclic isomers are also possible. For example:

6.8 a

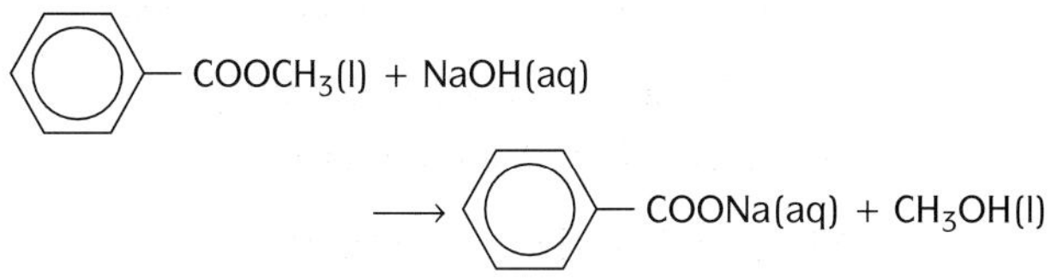

COOCH$_3$(l) + NaOH(aq)

⟶ COONa(aq) + CH$_3$OH(l)

b CH$_3$CH$_2$COOCH$_3$(l) + H$_2$O(l)
⟶ CH$_3$CH$_2$COOH(aq) + CH$_3$OH(l)

6.9 a Water; **b** esterification; **c** 3.

d

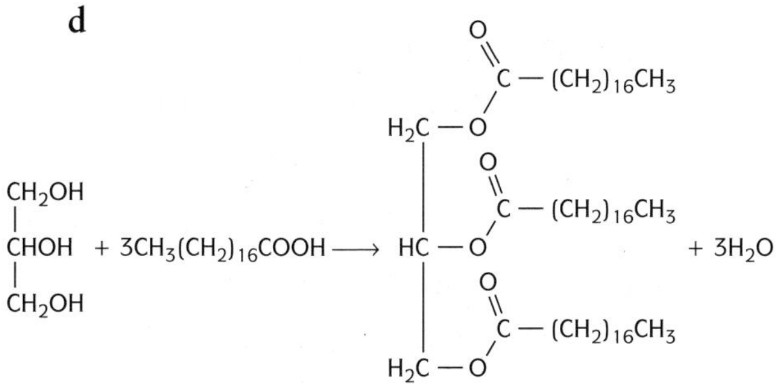

$$CH_2OH$$
$$CHOH + 3CH_3(CH_2)_{16}COOH \longrightarrow \cdots + 3H_2O$$
$$CH_2OH$$

Chapter 7

7.1 See *figure*.

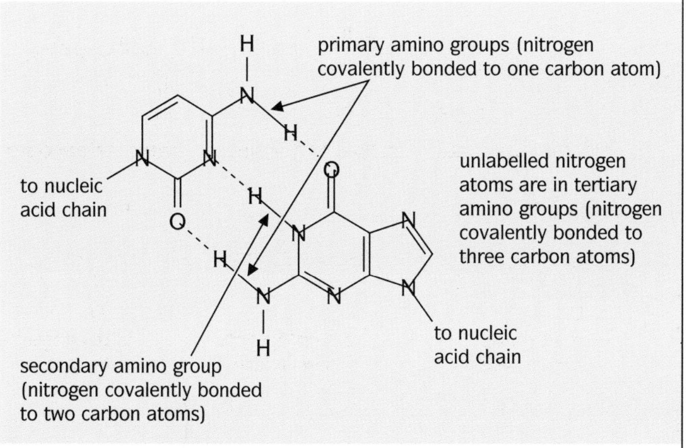

● **Answer for** SAQ 7.1

7.2

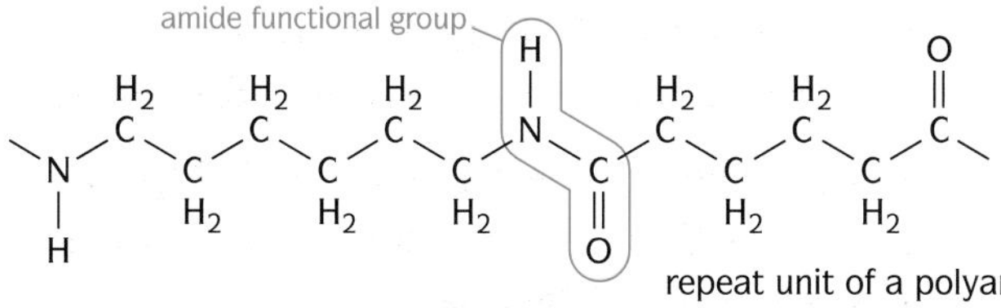

repeat unit of a polyamide

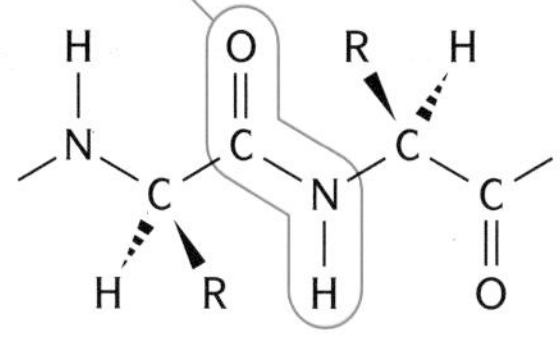

repeat unit of a protein

7.3 a Propylamine, CH$_3$CH$_2$CH$_2$NH$_2$.

b 4-aminophenol,

H$_2$N—⟨ ⟩—OH

7.4 a CH$_3$CH$_2$CH$_2$CH$_2$NH$_2$ + HNO$_3$
⟶ CH$_3$CH$_2$CH$_2$CH$_2$NH$_3^+$NO$_3^-$

b

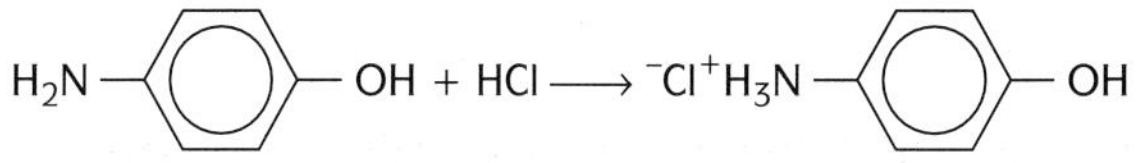

c

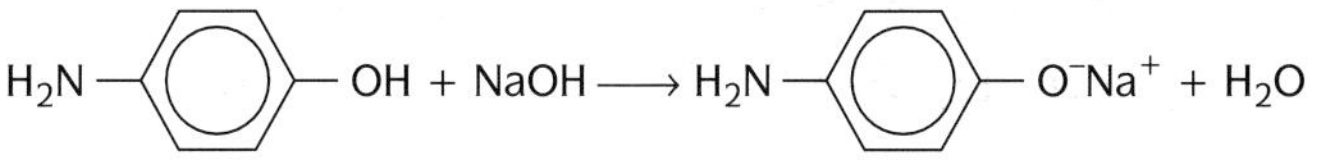

7.5

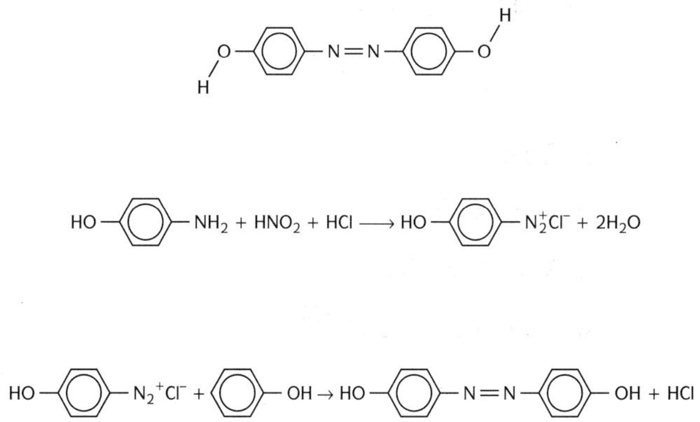

7.6 a

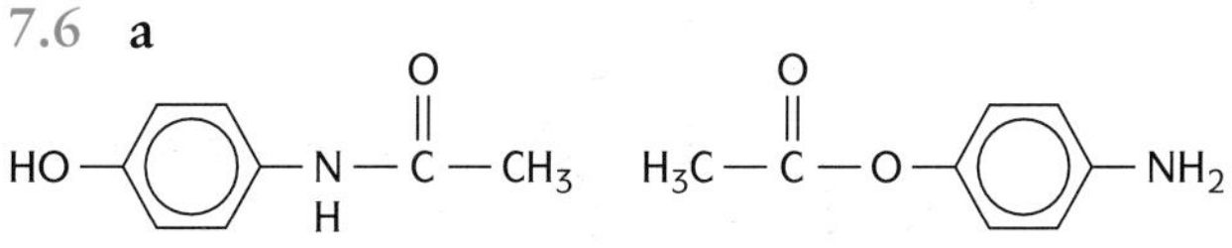

4-ethanoylaminophenol   4-aminophenyl ethanoate

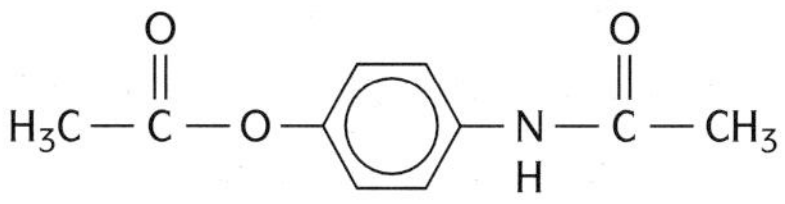

4-ethanoylaminophenyl ethanoate

b The products are propanoic acid, CH$_3$CH$_2$COOH, and an ammonium salt of the acid used. For example, hydrochloric acid gives ammonium chloride, NH$_4$Cl.

7.7 a (i) HOOCCH$_2$NH$_3^+$Cl$^-$(aq)

(ii) NH$_2$CH$_2$COO$^-$(aq)

b (i) HOOCCH$_2$NH$_2$(aq) + HCl(aq)
→ HOOCCH$_2$NH$_3^+$Cl$^-$(aq)

(ii) NH$_2$CH$_2$COOH(aq) + NaOH(aq)
→ NH$_2$CH$_2$COO$^-$Na$^+$(aq) + H$_2$O(l)

7.8 a

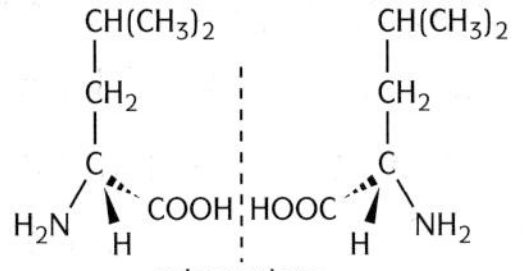

b

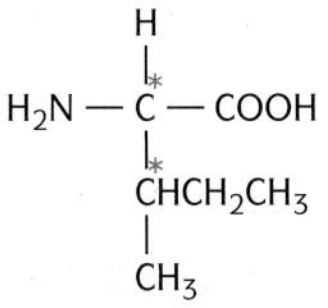

Chapter 8

8.1 a

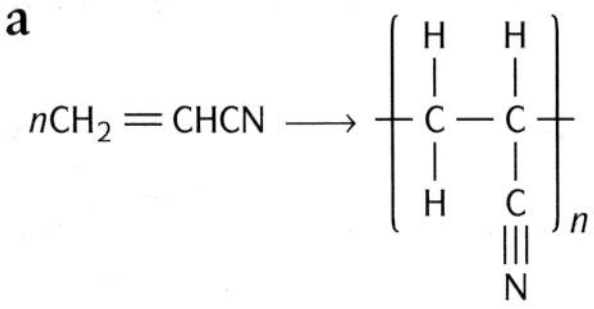

b (i)

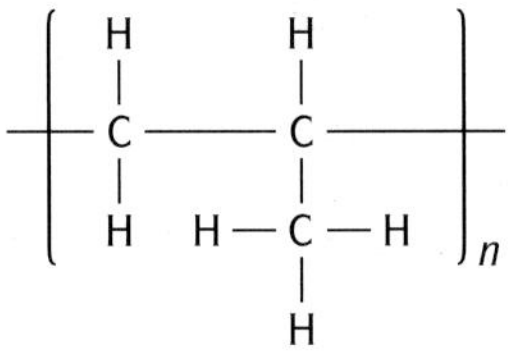

poly(propene)

(ii)

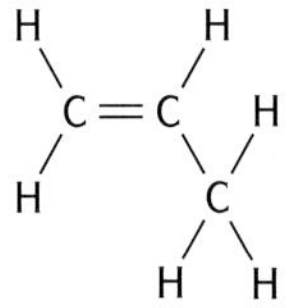

propene

8.2 Ethene, propene and other alkenes together with some longer chain alkanes might be formed on pyrolysis of poly(ethene). The alkenes could be used to make poly(alkene)s or other useful products (such as ethane-1,2-diol from ethene). The alkanes could be used to make petrol or diesel fuel.

8.3

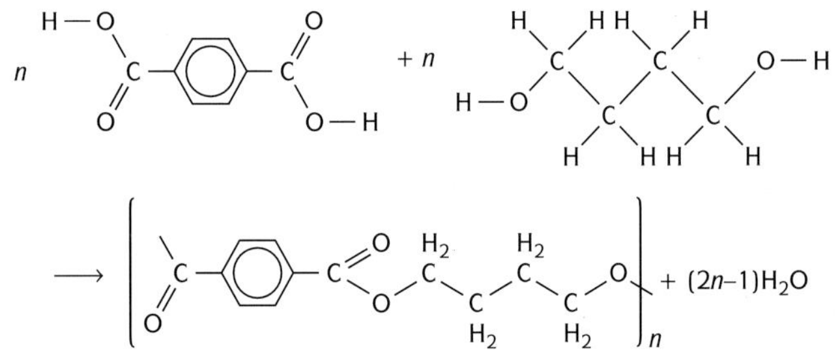

8.4

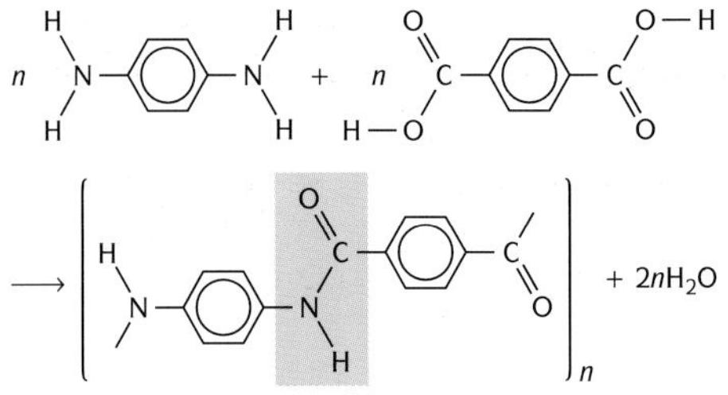

amide link

8.5 a

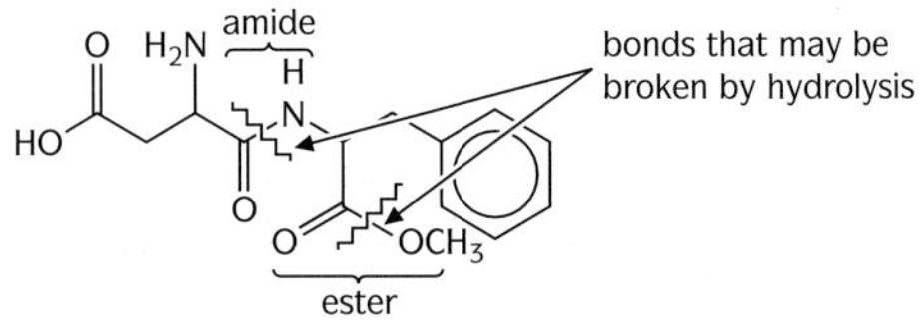

b

+ 2H$_2$O

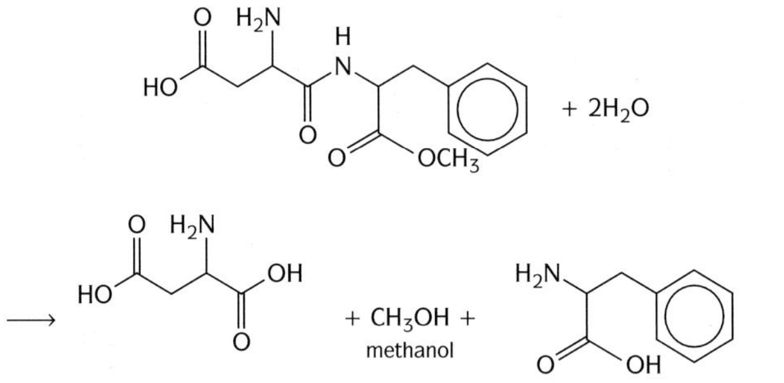

2-aminobutanedioic acid (aspartic acid)   + CH$_3$OH + methanol   2-amino-3-phenylpropanoic acid (phenylalanine)

Chapter 9

9.1 See *figure*.

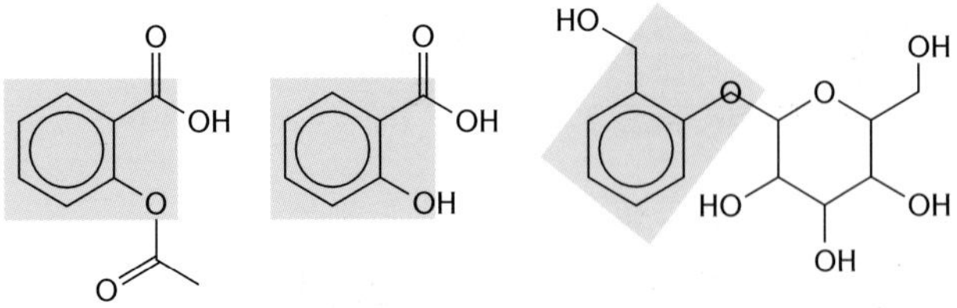

aspirin   2-hydroxybenzoic acid (salicylic acid)   salicin

● **Answer for** SAQ 9.1

9.2 A and **C**.

9.3 B.

9.4

a

$$H_2C=CH_2 \xrightarrow{\text{HCl(aq)}} CH_3CH_2Cl \xrightarrow[\text{under pressure}]{\text{heat with alcoholic ammonia}} CH_3CH_2NH_2$$

b

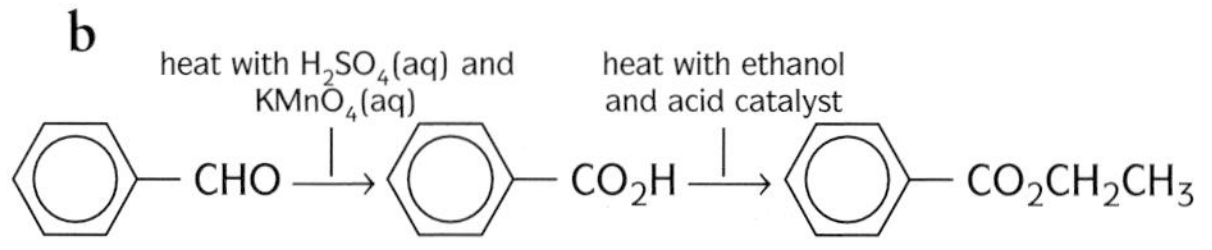

$$\bigcirc\text{—CHO} \xrightarrow[\text{KMnO}_4\text{(aq)}]{\text{heat with H}_2\text{SO}_4\text{(aq) and}} \bigcirc\text{—CO}_2\text{H} \xrightarrow[\text{and acid catalyst}]{\text{heat with ethanol}} \bigcirc\text{—CO}_2\text{CH}_2\text{CH}_3$$

c

$$CH_3CH_2CH_2Br \xrightarrow[\text{and ethanol}]{\text{reflux with NaCN(aq)}} CH_3CH_2CH_2CN \xrightarrow{\text{reflux with HCl(aq)}} CH_3CH_2CH_2CO_2H$$

d

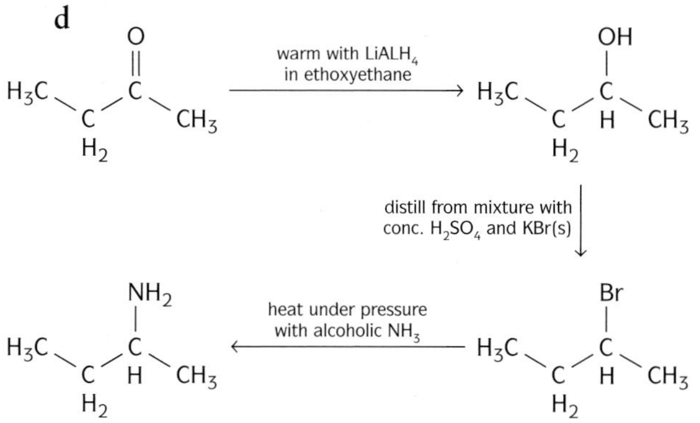

9.5

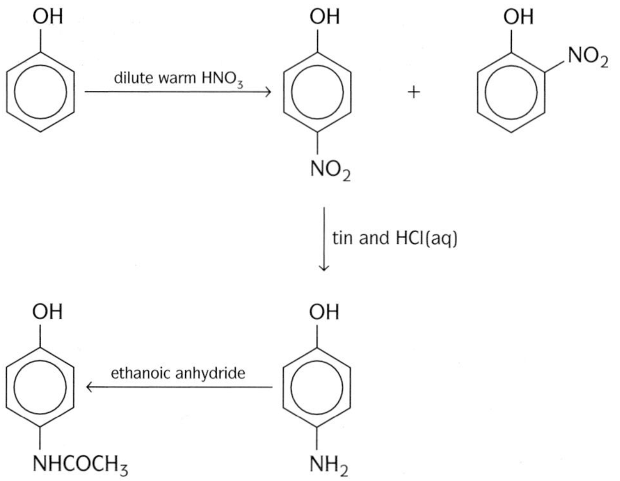

dilute warm HNO₃

tin and HCl(aq)

ethanoic anhydride

9.6 You might suggest:

AlCl₃(s) and CH₃COCl   (also 4- isomer)

reflux with H₂SO₄(aq) and KMnO₄(aq)

ethanoic anhydride

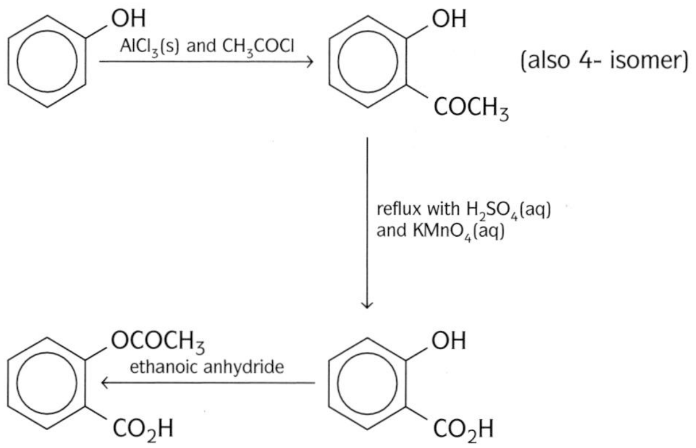

For the investigation:

1 Effect of temperature: try equal amounts of 2-hydroxybenzoic acid and ethanoic anhydride **a** with reflux and **b** without reflux.

2 Effect of a catalyst: repeat experiment **1** for each of the following acid catalysts (five drops of the catalyst are sufficient): **a** H_2SO_4, **b** H_3PO_4 and **c** CH_3CH_2OH.

3 Repeat experiments **1** and **2** to check the results.

4 Effect of changing concentration: repeat the experiment that gave the best yield, but this time use excess ethanoic anhydride. Repeat again with excess 2-hydroxybenzoic acid. Repeat this step to check the results.

9.7

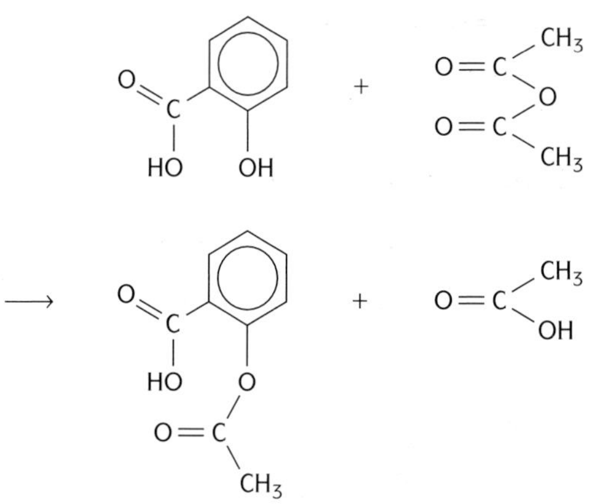

M_r for 2-hydroxybenzoic acid is 138; for ethanoic anhydride it is 102. Hence 2.0 g of 2-hydroxybenzoic acid require

$$\frac{102}{138} \times 2.0 = 1.48\,\text{g of ethanoic anhydride.}$$

Index (Numbers in italics refer to figures.)